When All Else Fails!

Unique, Last-Resort Strategies, Activities and Proven Programs for Reaching Difficult Students

By: Tom Carr

A C K N O W L E D G E M E N T S

Thanks to Aaron Carr, my son and fellow educator, for helping me put this book together. Not only did he assist with typing and editing, he also provided numerous suggestions.

I wish to acknowledge a new friend, Art Fettig. He provided me with three strategies and great poems. Art's website is www.artfettig.com.

Finally, I wish to thank the two principals at Cameron Park Elementary School in Hillsborough, North Carolina: Dr. Terry Rogers and Lisa Napp. They have been two of my biggest supporters.

CONTENTS

COLOR CODE YELLOW

COLOR CODE ORANGE

COLOR CODE RED

SPECIAL FEATURED STRATEGY

APPENDIX

When All Else Fails!

Unique, Last-Resort Strategies, Activities and Proven Programs for Reaching Difficult Students

ABOUT THE AUTHOR

Tom Carr lives in Hillsborough, North Carolina with his wife Carlye. He holds a Master's Degree in Counseling and Guidance from Syracuse University. Tom is a National Certified Counselor and a Licensed Professional Counselor. He has been a school counselor for over twenty years and presently is employed as an elementary school counselor for Orange County Schools in North Carolina. Tom also owns his own private practice, Carr Counseling and Consultation, Inc. and he is an education consultant and workshop presenter for Developmental Resources, Inc. in Chapin, South Carolina. In 1999 he created the Strength Coaching Foundation in his community which helps provide financial support for needy youth.

Tom has presented hundreds of workshops throughout the United States and Canada for teachers, counselors, and parents. He is the author of seven books.

INTRODUCTION
Use What Works For You, Change What Doesn't

Do you ever dread the first faculty meeting of the year? I often do because I know my principal has to inform the staff of all the changes for the new school year. As usual, there will be numerous changes, new programs, new testing requirements, adjustments to the curriculum, and there is always that "new" classroom management program that will surely put an end to all the discipline problems! Sometimes it is difficult to get excited and at other times it is easy to get frustrated when we are constantly bombarded with new ways to do things. There seems to be a lot of teaching "experts" at the State Department of Public Instruction telling us how to do things. Teachers tell me they wish those "experts" would leave them alone and let them teach. Their frustration reminds me of one of my favorite quotes:

"The beaver is very skilled at its craft.
It knows what to do to fix a dam. The
last thing it needs is for someone on the
bank shouting out dam instructions."
-anonymous

When it comes to change I am constantly reminded of another quote. Tom Jackson, one of the nation's leaders in Active Learning, says to teachers, "Use what works for you, change what doesn't." With the help of this book, I hope you continue to use the skills and tools that are effective in your class but, I also hope you are open to new ideas and changes presented in this book that can have a positive impact on your teaching and classroom management.

Let's not fear or resist change. Society is constantly changing and we have to keep up. As teachers, we realize that students are more challenging now than ever. Many of the strategies that were effective a few years ago are not appropriate today. So let's be open-minded and "change what doesn't work." Following is a list of 13 reasons "WHY SOME TEACHERS RESIST CHANGE." Check it out.

WHY SOME TEACHERS RESIST CHANGE:

1. **Fear of failure.** "I've tried four different discipline programs. What if this one doesn't work?"

2. **Procrastination.** "The timing just isn't right. Maybe I'll do it differently next year."

3. **That's not my style.** "My personality goes along with Authoritative Discipline. I'm just not into that new program. It's not strict enough."

4. **They lack awareness that change is needed.** "Sure, I've got a few discipline problems but, doesn't every teacher have a few?"

5. **Too busy.** "As teachers, we have a thousand things to do every day. Now the principals want me to try a new program."

6. **They get personal reinforcement for remaining the same.** "Jenny, thanks for listening to me. I needed to talk. You know I get the worst bunch of students every year!"

7. **Lack of support.** "That new idea looks good on paper, but are we getting the money and will the principal really be there to help out?"

8. **Low tolerance for change.** "I like the way things are. You know this is the way it's always been."

9. **They are Doubting Thomases.** "What makes you think that new program will be any better?"

10. **They are getting immune to change.** "I'm not going to get too involved or excited about this change because, as you know in education, there will be something different next year. We never stick with anything for more than a year or two!"

11. **They blame others.** "Why should I change? If parents were doing their jobs, we wouldn't have all these discipline problems."

12. **They deny responsibility.** "The principal is the one who should handle the discipline problems, not me. I'm supposed to teach."

13. **They want proof.** "Show me some proof first. I'm not changing to that new program until I see positive results from other schools."

HOW THIS BOOK CAN HELP

In my role as school counselor and consultant, I often have teachers who seek me out for advice on ways to assist them with their most difficult students. During these meetings the teachers will say something like this, "I've tried everything. Nothing seems to work. I need some new ideas." Yes, teachers are constantly in search of new ideas. During the past two or three years I have looked "high and low" for new, unique, and creative ideas. I've spent many long hours in my office trying to discover new strategies and quite often I experimented with them in my own school.

As the title of the book notes, *When All Else Fails*, I've developed "last resort" strategies to help teachers who have tried everything. The book contains not only 101 fresh approaches, but numerous reproducible sheets, stories, humor, checklists, poems, quotes, and other helpful bits of information. As you read the book and attempt to use some of the ideas, always keep in mind that not every strategy will work with every student. Some ideas that are effective with a first grader may not be successful with an eighth grader. As always, use your best judgment. WARNING: You may discover two or three strategies that you feel are too strong. If that happens, again, use your best judgment. Do not use anything that makes you feel uncomfortable. One other note, although this book focuses on students in grades K-8, most of the strategies are adaptable for students in high school.

As The Author, I Wouldn't Compromise

While writing this book I made a pledge not to go against my personal belief system when it comes to discipline. I will not waiver on these three beliefs:

1. **Avoid punishments as much as possible.** After reading numerous books by William Glasser and Alfie Kohn, I am convinced that in the long run, punishing children is seldom effective. My strategies are aimed at helping children become more responsible for their own actions.

2. **Limit rewards, candy, stickers and other "carrots."** Alfie Kohn's book, *Punished by Rewards: The Trouble with Gold Stars, Incentive Plans, A's, Praise and Other Bribes*, should be mandatory reading for all teachers.

3. **Do everything possible to keep difficult children in school.** I hope my strategies will help teachers keep those challenging students in school. Research shows over and over that out-of-school suspensions seldom work. I pray that my "last resort" ideas will save a few children. Yes, I do realize that we may not be able to keep every child in school. There are some extreme cases where children may have to be removed and placed in other settings.

Also, while putting this book together, I did my best to create ideas that supported Dr. William Glasser's "Seven Deadly Habits." In his book, *Every Student Can Succeed*, he advises parents and teachers to avoid:

- criticizing
- blaming
- complaining
- nagging
- threatening
- punishing
- rewarding to control

(p.7)

HOW TO USE THIS BOOK

This book is divided into five sections based on a color code. The colors include: green, blue, yellow, orange and red. The "softer" colors of green and blue contain low level interventions while the "louder" colors of orange and red involve more extreme measures. The book should be read in order from green all the way up to red. The thought here is that you should always start with the lowest level of intervention and work your way up. Many of the orange and red strategies will only work provided that the green and blue strategies were attempted first. DO NOT GO STRAIGHT TO THE RED SECTION AND IMPLEMENT THE STRATEGIES. Again, start at green.

Although you'll find this book useful any time during the year, it will prove most effective as part of program that is started at the beginning of the year. Sometimes it is very difficult to implement new strategies in March or April.

The Color Codes

Green:
This section includes many preventive measures to use in your classroom. It includes thoughts on the importance of teachers working as a team as well as information on helping parents. Green also refers to those students who are consistently well-behaved and who rarely, if ever, have to be corrected.

Blue:
Blue students are usually well-behaved. They may "slip off the track" once in a while but are usually corrected with simple reminders.

Yellow:
Strategies in this section will help you with students whom you are beginning to have some concerns. They are still quite manageable, but at times you have to take action (i.e. use time-out, call parents, write plans/contracts, take away a privilege). These students disrupt class on occasion. The yellow student's behavior can be like a roller-coaster ride; some days fine and other days terrible.

Orange:
This color code refers to those students who cause you much concern. These students not only disrupt class often, but they also eat up a lot of your energy. On the positive side, you do see some potential for improvement.

Red:
Students in this group are quite unmanageable most of the time. They can be aggressive, verbally abusive, openly defiant, or refuse to do any work. Last resort strategies are needed as well as help from support personnel. We're not giving up on these kids, but we are realistic as well; they may need more help than the school can provide.

Don't Forget… Positive Change Is A Marathon, Not A Sprint

As you use these strategies in this book, keep in mind that positive change takes time. Seldom is there a quick-fix. Be patient and keep trying. I remember Dr. William Glasser saying at one of his presentations, "If you want to change your school from an average one to a "Quality School," it will take three to five years." Don't give up on these kids and always look for those little signs that show progress is being made. Yes, there is light at the end of the tunnel. I'll finish this section with a true story about a seventh grade teacher who was able to see a tiny bit of progress in the middle of a bad situation.

As Mrs. Harrington began her fifth period Social Studies class she noticed that a teacher-observation specialist from central office sat down in the back of the room. Although this caused her to be a little nervous, she started her lesson. Ten minutes into her lesson, six-foot, three-inch, Jason started acting up. When he would not settle down she asked him to move to the "cool-down" chair. As he walked in front of the class he mumbled the "F" word three or four times and then threw himself into the chair. Mrs. Harrington did not say anything and continued to teach. At the end of the lesson the teacher-observer asked Mrs. Harrington, "Why didn't you do anything when that big student cursed?" Mrs. Harrington calmly replied, "I didn't do anything at that time because I was happy." The observer then asked, "What do you mean by that?" Mrs. Harrington smiled and said, "Two weeks ago when I told him to go to the "cool-down" chair, he picked it up and threw it out the window and was suspended for two weeks. So today, when I asked him to move, the worst thing he did was curse. I said to myself, 'Hey, he's making progress!'

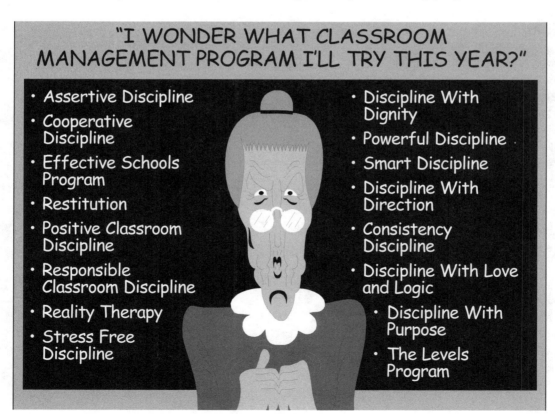

"I WONDER WHAT CLASSROOM MANAGEMENT PROGRAM I'LL TRY THIS YEAR?"

- Assertive Discipline
- Cooperative Discipline
- Effective Schools Program
- Restitution
- Positive Classroom Discipline
- Responsible Classroom Discipline
- Reality Therapy
- Stress Free Discipline

- Discipline With Dignity
- Powerful Discipline
- Smart Discipline
- Discipline With Direction
- Consistency Discipline
- Discipline With Love and Logic
- Discipline With Purpose
- The Levels Program

STRATEGY #1
Class Conduct Color Codes

At the start of the school year add the names of your students to the Class Conduct Color Code Sheets (see next page). At the end of each month, take a few minutes to color in the appropriate color (green, blue, yellow, orange, red) based on their behavior. This sheet/chart will be very useful for several reasons:

● Your September ratings may give you an idea of the difficulties/challenges this class may present. If you have a lot of yellows and oranges in September, can you decrease the number by the end of the year?

● The color coding provides a very "visual" tool to share with parents.

● Teachers may want to compare color codes of students. For instance, Jerry may have a rating of orange in Math but in art class he has a rating of green.

● The coding may make you aware of slow changes in a child's behavior that cause concerns about emotional issues, home problems, etc. Let's say that Ellen was a green in September and October, then a blue in November, and in December she reaches yellow, then you may want to investigate.

● The color coding will help you mark the effect one student has on the whole class. If your most difficult student transfers out of your class, does his removal increase the numbers of blues and greens? Or, on the other hand, if two new, well-behaved students move in, does their presence cause other students to adjust to their behaviors?

● Put on your thinking cap. Get creative. There are many more ways to use this sheet that will help both you and your students.

Class Conduct Color Code Sheet

Student	Sep	Oct	Nov	Dec	Jan	Feb	Mar	Apr	May	Jun	Jul	Aug

COLOR CODING RATING SCALE

Green: Behavior is consistently excellent. Rarely has to be corrected.

Blue: Overall, behavior is good. Slips off tract once in a while but is corrected with simple reminders.

Yellow: I have some concerns here. Still quite manageable. Occasionally I have to take action (i.e. timeout, call parents, write contracts, conference with student).

Orange: Very concerned here. He/she is taking up much of my time and energy. Causes several disruptions a week but most of the time I am able to make some progress. The child has potential to improve.

Red: Quite often this student is very unmanageable. He/she constantly affects my teaching and the learning of others. Serious action is needed to help this student.

STRATEGY #2
A Quiet Pause for Prayers and Affirmations

Before getting out of bed, in the shower, at breakfast, in the car, or in the school's parking lot, pause to say a prayer or repeat a positive affirmation before facing the students. Pausing for prayer or using reassuring self-talk throughout the day can be a blessing and, everyone knows, we need all the help we can get sometimes!

Many teachers respond to this strategy by saying that they are too busy to find a time to pause for a prayer. I say, "Find the time!" I love what the minister, lecturer, and counselor Hugh Prather writes about the importance of making time for prayer in a busy world. In his book, *Spiritual Notes to Myself*, he says, "If you lose your peace, break with the situation. If you need to pray, pray now. 'Oh, but that might be too awkward or too much trouble,' we say to ourselves. But if we had diarrhea, we would break with the situation. We would get up from the meeting. We would pull the car off the road. We would put down the phone. We would get out of line. We would excuse ourselves from dinner. It's very simple: All we have to is make the peace of God as important as we make diarrhea." (p. 130).

Here are five of my favorite affirmations. They come from Bo Lozoff's book, *It's a Meaningful Life*.

1. "May my behavior today express my deepest beliefs."

2. "May I approach each and every task today with quiet impeccability."

3. "May I be a simple, humble, kind presence on the earth today."

4. "May I be grateful today to those who came before me, and may I make the roads smoother for those who travel after me."

5. "May I leave each place at least a little better than I found it today." (p. 31)

STRATEGY #3
The Declaration of Inter-dependence

Although, every school has challenging students, not every teacher agrees on the best way to discipline them. Regardless of their differing views and opinions, teachers need to remain professional in how they interact with the students and their co-workers. Author and motivational speaker, Art Fettig has devised a special document for teachers called the Declaration of Inter-dependence for Teachers (see next page). By signing the Declaration, teachers agree not only to support each other but, to also positively interact with co-workers who conduct themselves in ways that may not be professional or in ways that are contrary to the school's mission/belief statement. I encourage all schools to sign and post the declaration.

STRATEGY #4
15 Behaviors for Building Respect

On a regular basis, review the checklist, **"15 Behaviors for Building Mutual Respect between Teacher and Student."**

AS A TEACHER, DO YOU ....?

____ 1. Call on everyone in the room equitably

____ 2. Provide individual help

____ 3. Give an appropriate/fair amount of "wait time"

____ 4. Ask questions to help give students clues about the answer

____ 5. Ask questions that require more thought than just a yes or no response

____ 6. Tell students whether their answers are right or wrong

____ 7. Give praise that is specific and not phony

____ 8. Give reasons for praise

____ 9. Truly listen

____ 10. Accept the feelings of the student

____ 11. Get within an arm's length of each student every day

____ 12. Show kindness and courtesy to students

____ 13. Show personal interest and give compliments

____ 14. Make attempts to appropriately touch students (i.e. handshake, pat on back)

____ 15. Ignore or not call to attention every misbehavior

*checklist adapted from the Los Angeles Board of Education's "Teacher Expectations and Student Achievement."

Declaration Of Inter-Dependence For Teachers

When in the course of human events, it becomes necessary for an organization and its members to make a total uncompromising commitment to excellence for the good of all,

And whereas, we do hereby resolve that we will do all in our power, every moment of every day to make excellence in education a value we hold dear, in our planning and in the fulfillment of other goals and activities.

Therefore, we do hereby declare and acknowledge our inter-dependence upon one another, for the pursuit of excellence in both a personal and mutual obligation.

We are human, you and I, and in our pursuit for excellence we truly need the support of one another.

I promise I will positively inter-act when I believe that your performance might result in anything but that excellence we mutually seek.
And I hereby personally request that you will positively interact with me when you see me acting in a less than professional manner, for our mutual good and for the good of each and every student.

Therefore, for the support of this Declaration, we mutually pledge our best professional efforts, continuing respect for our mutual goals and for one another, and a commitment to excellence at our school.

Name of School_____ Date_____

Signature of principal (s) _____

_____

_____

Developed by Art Fettig, 1994: Used With Permission.

SIGNATURES
DECLARATION OF INTER-DEPENDENCE

Name of School _____ Date _____

STRATEGY #5
Create a Set of Class Mottoes

Sometime during the first week or two of school, ask each of your students to create a personal motto. Encourage them to come up with mottoes that help them personally get through life. Also, you may suggest that their mottoes provide other students with advice and encouragement. Then post all their mottoes on the wall. Throughout the remainder of the year have your students refer to the list. What makes this list so powerful is that the list is developed by the students, not adults. For example, instead of saying to the class, "I think most of you are getting behind in your work," say, "What's Helen's motto say?" Helen's motto may say something like, "The longer you put off doing a job, the harder it becomes."

Don't forget to create your own personal motto and share it with your students. Lately, my motto has been, "All days are good, but some are better than others." Here are a few clever mottoes written by Amish students in Pennsylvania around 1960.

● I am only me, but I am still someone.

● I cannot do everything, but I can do something.

● Even though our minds may work slower than some children's, let us bear in mind that it is only a blessing that they work at all.

● Let us pray not for lighter burdens, but for stronger backs.

● Remember when you talk you only repeat what you already know; but if you listen you may learn something.

● We are known by our actual deeds and not what we boast we can do.

● Singing is a pleasant pastime, good exercise for the lungs and a nice way of giving praise to God.

● You can be pleasant without talking a lot. Think twice before you speak once.

● Never, never be afraid to do what's right, even if all others are doing wrong.

STRATEGY #6
Climb Down From Your Control Tower

Have you ever entered a classroom in which the students were actively engaged and there was a positive "buzz" in the air but, you couldn't tell if the teacher was there? Then you looked around and saw the teacher almost "camouflaged" in the mix of young bodies. Effective teachers are not overly concerned about being in control or in charge. They tend to be what William Glasser calls, lead teachers. Lead teachers are not coercive, threatening, loud and punitive. They teach by guiding, coaching, encouraging, and they teach children to be responsible for their own behaviors.

If your belief is that you must control students, you may find yourself hitting a brick wall. Climb down from your control tower and mix with the students.

The following paragraph is one of the most powerful ones I've ever read on trying to be in control or always taking charge. Alfie Kohn makes some very strong points in his book, *What to Look for in the Classroom*.

Students are far less likely to act aggressively, intrusively, or obnoxiously in places where the teacher is not concerned about being in charge — and, indeed, is not particularly interested in classroom-management techniques. I realized that the discipline problems I experienced with some of my own classes were not a function of children who were insufficiently controlled but of a curriculum that was insufficiently engaging. (The students weren't trying to make my life miserable; they were trying to make the time pass faster.) It occurred to me that books on discipline almost never raise the possibility that when a student doesn't do what he is told, the problem may be with what he has been told to do – or to learn. (Kohn, 1998 p.14)

STRATEGY #7
No Violence Contract

Sometime during the first week or two of the school year, encourage your students to sign the "No Violence Contract." (See next page) Post the contract on the wall.

NO VIOLENCE
CONTRACT

- I pledge to do everything within my power to control my behavior.

- I will not allow my behavior to get to the point where I physically hurt myself or others.

- I also agree to do my best to use the conflict resolution skills and anger management strategies that are taught in this class.

Class Signatures:

Teacher Signature _____ *Date* _____

STRATEGY #8
It's Never OK!

This is a very effective tool to use with younger students when introducing topics such as non-violence and conflict resolution. The following is an example of how a teacher, Mr. Harris, uses it with first graders.

1. Mr. Harris stands at the front of his class. He takes his index finger and waves it back and forth and says, "It's never OK to....

2. He then takes his index and middle finger and touches his arm and finishes his sentence..."to hurt anyone's body...

3. He then takes his two fingers and touches his heart and says, "to hurt anyone's feelings...

4. He then takes his two hands and pretends to break a pencil and says, "or to hurt anyone's property."

He has the students repeat the words and go through the finger/hand movements every morning. "It's never OK to hurt anyone's body, anyone's feelings, or anyone's property." If a child does hurt another student, he/she is asked, "What did we say about 'It's never OK?'" Then the child must go through the movements and repeat the rules.

STRATEGY #9
Silence is Golden

Students need to learn appropriate ways of communicating with others without talking. By learning quiet communication skills, the classroom will be more peaceful. As a class, develop a chart of quiet communication skills. Practice the skills. Examples can include the following:

- Hand raised in the air with index finger up means, "Teacher, I need help."
- Hand raised with two fingers: "Teacher, may I go to the bathroom?"
- Index finger to the lips: "Be quiet, please."
- Arm extended straight out, palm forward, fingers up: "Stop."
- Fingers in and thumb up: "Good job!"
- Waving index finger and wearing frown: "No, no."
- Leaning forward with hand cupped behind ear: "Speak up, please."

You can create many other signs/signals to use. Three or four times a week, place a gold-covered sign up on the front wall that reads, "Silence is Golden." When the sign is up, students are not to use words. Instead they are to use the quiet communication skills they've learned.

STRATEGY #10
The Golden Rule

Have you ever asked your students, "How many of you know The Golden Rule?" I am amazed by the number of students who don't! Find the time to discuss the rule on a regular basis and post it somewhere in the room. Mention it when students have conflicts. Remember The Golden Rule:

"Treat other people the way you would like them to treat you."

STRATEGY #11
Aristotle's Golden Mean

There is an old rule of conduct known as Aristotle's Golden Mean. It encourages people to travel the middle road between being nonassertive and aggressive. The middle road is called assertiveness. As teachers, we realize that children need to be assertive at times. Obviously, they must know the difference between aggressiveness and assertiveness. Somewhere in your room post the Basic Assertive Rights (see next page). Review them often throughout the year.

STRATEGY #12
"Hey, Be Quiet! She's Sitting on Her Throne."

A quick glance in *Webster's New Dictionary* finds that the word "throne" means "a chair of state richly ornamented and raised, seat of a bishop in the church of his diocese; sovereign power." In the old days, whenever a ruler, king, queen, or church leader sat on the throne, the people would stop what they were doing and listen quietly for an important message. These events were very infrequent.

Think about creating your own, specially designed and decorated throne (chair). You may also want to have your robe and crown hanging on the wall next to the chair. Whenever you have a real important message for your students (good news or bad news) don your robe and crown and head to the throne. Since you rarely do this, the students become quiet and wait for the message.

This is a neat attention-getter. There are two important keys to success. First, make your visits to the throne rare (once or twice a month). If you use it too often, it loses its spontaneity/uniqueness. Secondly, use the throne for both good and not-so-good announcements. If you only use it for negative communication, the students will not be as excited.

BASIC ASSERTIVE RIGHTS
As a person, you hold the following rights:

1. The right to act in ways that promote your dignity and self respect as long as others' rights are not violated in the process

2. The right to be treated with respect

3. The right to say "No" and not feel guilty

4. The right to experience and express your feelings

5. The right to take time to slow down and think

6. The right to change you mind

7. The right to ask for what you want

8. The right to do less than you are humanly capable of doing

9. The right to ask for information

10. The right to make mistakes

11. The right to feel good about yourself.

Source: Jakubowski, P. and Lange, A.J. (1978). The Assertive Option: Your Rights and Responsibilities. Champaign, IL: Research Press Co. 80-81

STRATEGY #13
Bring On the Zamboni

Have you ever been to a professional hockey game? Have you noticed that at the end of each period a large tractor-like machine comes out and cleans the ice? That big machine is called a Zamboni™. This impressive machine clears away any debris that has fallen on the ice, repairs/patches up holes and uneven areas, and leaves a thin layer of water that helps form a new surface of ice for the next period. Every period in hockey starts with a clean, smooth playing surface.

As teachers we can have challenging days, or sometimes just a difficult period. I've often heard teachers say something like, "Oh, my fifth period Social Studies group is really getting to me." We need to look at each group of students or each period as if they were a period of a hockey game. When one period ends, we need to bring on our imaginary Zamboni™ to get the playing surface ready for the next period. Just because the fifth period students were rude, should you take it out on the sixth period students? Just like we start each day with a clean slate, we should start each period in a positive way.

There is a "hockey nut" teacher in New York who actually keeps a toy Zamboni™ on his desk. As soon as one period of students leaves, he drives his Zamboni™, with lights and sirens going, across his desk as a visual reminder to get ready for the next period.

STRATEGY #14
Three Tricks for Tempering Playground Chaos

Most teachers realize the importance of taking their students outside for fresh air, play, and to burn off some energy. But, quite often I hear these same teachers make comments like this, "Sometimes I dread taking them outside because they argue, fight, tattle, and get so "wound-up" that it takes a long time to get them settled down and back to work." Here are some tricks or strategies that will help eliminate a great number of playground problems.

1. **Play with the kids.** Students enjoy playing ball, jumping rope, or participating in a game of four-square with their teachers. A special relationship builds between a student and a teacher when they play together outside. As far back as 1909, Jessie H. Bancroft was quoted as saying, "The teacher should never hesitate to participate in the play of children. Nothing can quickly gain the respect and affection of a child than such participation."

There are other benefits to being active on the playground. First, there are safety issues. You can prevent many accidents. Secondly, you can help children learn rules, play fair, and teach skills. You can also teach a lot of character education on the playground. Playing fair, sportsmanship, respect, compassion, honesty, courage, perseverance and other important traits can be learned outside.

2. **Make it a rule in your class that when playing team sports outside that no one is allowed to keep score.** Encourage students that when playing kick ball, basketball, or softball that they should just play for the fun of it. It is not important which team wins. So many fights occur in competitive games at recess.

3. **Make sure that when selecting students to be on a team or when grouping them for other games you stay away from picking two captains to choose who they want on their teams.** I've seen much pain, hurt, and loss of self-esteem on playgrounds when kids gather around to be chosen by the two captains. That hurt and pain often carries over into the classroom. I recommend keeping a copy of Angelyn Hall's poem, *"Choosing Sides"* somewhere in your class. (see next page) Make sure you and your students read it often.

STRATEGY #15
The Big Bopper

In my office I keep a very large, inflatable hammer called The Big Bopper. Quite often I take it with me to classes when I do my guidance lessons. At the end of the lesson I might say, "I hope you students understood the important lesson today. To make sure you don't forget it, I'm going to pound the message into your head." Then I go around the room and lightly bop each student on the head. Fifth graders get just as much of a kick out of this as do the kindergarteners. On days that I don't bring The Big Bopper to class, the students seem disappointed. I truly believe that my "attention-getter" has helped many students remember my lessons and it has helped me build a closer relationship with the students. They love getting bopped! You may want to consider adding a unique "attention-getter" for your room.

Choosing Sides

By Angelyn Hall

Thick-rimmed glasses
Masking tape across the nose-piece
Frail stature, skinny legs —
Portrait of a nine-year-old.

It was that time again,
Worst day of every week.
The day they'd play softball in Pys. Ed.
The day he'd often pleaded to stay home,
Feigning an illness — any illness,
Waking up early to drink hot coffee
To raise his temperature above the normal mark —
But his mom knew the trick.

So now he stood there,
Hands in pockets,
Shuffling his feet,
Waiting to hear his name.

Wondering if anyone else would also hear
The sound of his heart beating
As he waited for his name.

Choosing teams and knowing he'd be last,
Not even his friends would want him.
Please, don't let him be last again.
Didn't they know he'd practiced,
How he could catch so much better now?

Yet he knew the outcome all too well —
There'd be no one left but him.
Then they'd snicker and shake their heads
Saying loudly — as if he wasn't standing right there —
"You take him."
"No, you. We don't want to lose."
They, ignorant of their own cruelty — or maybe not.
And he'd hang his head,
Knowing all his classmates had heard his public humiliation —
His silent walk to the gallows.

Who was the unfeeling human
Who'd started the practice of choosing sides?
Oh destroyer of self-esteem.
Ten to one — he'd never been a little boy
Who'd stood there waiting for his name.

poem used with permission of the author

STRATEGY #16
Let's Go Back to 1848

Here's an idea for a fun and valuable lesson. Share a copy of the rules from a North Carolina school that were used in 1848 (see page 28). Begin a discussion and watch the excitement grow. Here are a few questions to get you going.

- Does anyone know what "lashes" are?
- Have you noticed how spelling was different? Why was that?
- According to the rules, were boys and girls punished equally?
- What do these words mean? blackgarding, bandy, trab ball, Heart Lesson?
- Why do you think children weren't allowed to swing?
- How many rules do you see that deal with respecting adults?
- Look at rule #8. How many lashes would a boy get if he climbed ten feet up a tree?
- Why do you suppose it was a more serious violation to get caught playing cards than it was to get caught drinking "spirituous liquors?"
- Do you think children should be punished for not saying, "Yes, Sir/Marm."?
- Would these rules be effective in our schools today?

STRATEGY #17
Give Me a Break, Give Me a Break!

There's an old television commercial that reminds us to change our oil and oil filter in our cars often. If we don't, we may need to buy a new transmission later. The commercial has a mechanic who warns us, "You can pay me now or you can pay me later." I think the same theory can be compared to the importance of students getting an appropriate amount of recess, play, or breaks during the day. If they don't get a break or two, both teacher and student will "pay later" as teaching and learning begins to suffer.

Even in the early 1900's, educators realized the importance of breaks. In 1910, George Ellsworth Johnson noted, "In the first place, have a recess. All need it, particularly the bad boy, more particularly still the good but anaemic girl. And the teacher needs it, in a certain sense more than they." In 1912, teacher Mabel Carney said, "When things have gone so far that the children become languid and sleepy, it is time for action. Open the windows to their very limit. Let the children march, run, play leap frog, or do almost anything requiring bodily exertion, while the room is thoroughly flushed with pure air."

So, what does the latest research say about the need for recess? Olga Jarrett and Darlene Maxwell (2000) uncovered this provocative information:

- Children are more fidgety when recess is delayed.
- Students are more off task when recess does not occur.

- Student recall is improved when learning is spaced rather than presented all at once.
- Brain research on attention found that; a) the brain cannot maintain attention for long periods of time, requiring contrast (such as a new location or novel stimuli) to regain attention; b) for information to be processed, down time is needed to recycle chemicals crucial for long-term memory function; c) attention is cyclical, involving 90-110 minute rhythmical patterns throughout the day.
- Extensive studies on fourth graders find that they were less on task and fidgety in the classroom on days when they had no recess.
- Hyperactive children benefit the most from breaks and recess.

Make sure you and your students get regular breaks. At first it may appear that you are getting behind in schoolwork, but you'll more than make it up later as children are given time to "recharge" their batteries.

Strategy #18
A "Timely" Discipline Referral Form

Many schools throughout the country are focusing on Character Education. Characteristics such as respect for authority, self-control, trustworthiness, honesty and citizenship are stressed in ways to help students become self-disciplined. In spite of the valiant efforts of teachers, some students still get in trouble and have to be sent to the office. I suggest that if schools have a student referral/discipline form, they implement Character Education aspects on the form (see page 29). A student who is sent to the office probably knows he was sent there for hitting but, does he know which character trait he ignored? Instead of the principal concentrating on the issue of hitting, he can discuss the character aspects of the student's actions. The student still has to deal with the consequences of his behavior, but the focus of the incident is more positive and hopefully the student will make quicker progress in changing behaviors.

Strategy # 19
Changing the World, One Story at a Time

One of my favorite motivational speakers and storytellers is Dan Clark. He uses the slogan, "Changing the world, one story at a time." I strongly agree with the slogan. Behaviors, attitudes, and self-esteem can be changed by powerful stories. I've made storytelling a big part of my counseling program. I encourage you to become a storyteller. I also encourage you to focus on true stories. I believe that children today are bombarded with too much fiction and they have trouble separating what is real and what is not. Effective non-fiction stories can make a difference.

Oh-How Times Have Changed

A list of punishments as published and used in 1848 in a North Carolina school

NO.	RULES OF SCHOOL	LASHES
1.	Boys and girls playing together	4
2	Quareling	4
3.	Fighting	5
4.	Fighting at school	5
5.	Quareling at school	3
6.	Gambling or betting at school	4
7.	Playing cards at school	10
8.	Climbing for every foot over three feet up a tree	1
9.	Telling lies	7
10.	Telling tales out of school	8
11.	Nick naming each other	4
12.	Giving each other ill names	3
13.	Fighting each other in time of Books	2
14.	Swaring at school	8
15.	Blackgarding each other	6
16.	For misbehaving to girls	10
17.	For leaving school without leave of the teacher	4
18.	For going home with each other without leave of the teacher	4
19.	For drinking spirituous liquors at school	8
20.	Making swings and swinging on them	7
21.	For misbehaving when a stranger is in the house	6
22.	For waring long finger nailes	2
23.	For not making a bow when a stranger comes in or goes out	3
24.	Misbehaving to persons on the road	4
25.	For not making a bow when you meet a person	4
26.	For going to girl's play places	3
27.	For going to boy's play places	2
28.	Coming to school with dirty face and hands	2
29.	For calling each other liars	4
30.	For playing Bandy	10
31.	For blotting your copy book	2
32.	For not making a bow when you go home and when you come away	4
33.	Wrestling at school	4
34.	Scuffling at school	4
35.	For not making a bow when going out to go home	2
36.	For weting each other washing at play time	2
37.	Girls going to boy's play places	2
38.	For hallowing and hooping going home	3
39.	For delaying time going home or coming to school	4
40.	For not making a bow when you come in or go out	2
41.	For throwing anything harder than your trab ball	4
42.	For every word you mis in your Heart Lesson without good excuse	1
43.	For not saying yes Sir and no Sir or yes marm or no marm	2
44.	For troubleing each others writing affares	2
45.	For not washing at play time when going to Books	4
46.	For going and playing about the mill or creek	6
47.	For going about the barn or doing any mischief about the place	7

Student Discipline Referral Form

Student Name _____ Grade_____

Person Sending Student _____

Time Student was Sent _____ Date_____

Please check the character trait(s) which the student did not display.

___ Citizenship   ___ Responsibility   ___ Patience

___ Respect for Others   ___ Fairness   ___ Tolerance

___ Civility   ___ Self Control   ___ Respect for Authority

___ Respect for Property   ___ Honesty   ___ Trustworthiness

___ Cooperation   ___ Sportsmanship   ___ Respect for Learning

Write a brief description of the student's misbehavior _____

_____

_____

_____

_____

Action taken by administrator _____

_____

_____

_____

_____

Administrator's signature _____

Try this amazing story on your class and then begin a discussion.

Booker T. Washington's Most Important Lesson

Booker T. Washington, the great black educator, founded the Tuskegee Institute in Alabama in the 1880's. I'm sure he taught many lessons at his institute but probably his most important was taught, not in a classroom, but while walking along a road.

Although President Lincoln abolished slavery in the 1860's, many blacks were still being mistreated twenty years later. One day, Booker T. Washington was passing a beautiful mansion owned by a wealthy white family. The mistress of the house saw him walking by. She did not know who he was and yelled to him, "Hey, you, chop me a pile of firewood right now!" He could have gotten angry and said no. Instead, he calmly took off his jacket and tie. Several hours later, he went back to the front door and told her he had finished. He handed the mistress the axe and left. As he was leaving, one of her servants said, "Ma'am, that man was Professor Washington!"

The next day, the embarrassed mistress went to Washington to apologize. He responded, "It's entirely all right, Madam. I like to work and I'm delighted to do favors for my friends." He created a new friend and this new friend ended up donating thousands of dollars to his needy institute.

NOTE: See the appendix for two bonus stories.

STRATEGY # 20
The Best Parent's Daily Checklist Ever?

As we all know, teachers and parents must work together as a team in order to have children who are successful, both behaviorally and academically. While most of this book focuses on behavior, we can't overlook schoolwork and homework. Several years ago, the American Association of Parents and Children developed the best checklist I've found (see next page). It was designed for parents and offered several unique strategies to help their children become better learners.

I recommend sending home a copy to each parent sometime during the first week of school. If possible, pass out copies at the first parent gathering of the year. It wouldn't hurt to send out additional copies at the end of each marking period.

Your Child's Learning:
A Daily Checklist

___ 1. Is a "quiet time" for learning scheduled for my child today?

___ 2. What opportunities can I take advantage of to praise the initiative or thinking of my child?

___ 3. Have I clearly expressed my expectations and avoided making excuses for low effort by my child?

___ 4. Have I in some way motivated my child to learn today by rewarding or praising good effort?

___ 5. What will I read or write today to set a good example?

___ 6. How will I get relaxed before working on homework with my child so that I do not get frustrated and impatient.

___ 7. Have I made it clear that my child (not me) is responsible for homework?

___ 8. Can I involve my child in a household activity today that will show the practical importance of learning?

___ 9. Can I encourage my child to pursue a hobby, read the newspaper, or another independent activity?

___10. Did I remember to "sign off" on homework and attach a note if there is a problem?

Source: American Association of Parents and Children, McLean VA.

STRATEGY #21
Individual Student Color Code Cards

Give each student a set of five cards. Use the same color code system that is being used in this book: green, blue, yellow, orange, and red. Encourage the students to always have one of the colored cards on the corner of their desks. Depending on which color card they use, it will provide you and other students with information on how they are feeling.

Let's look at how Lisa, third grader, would use her cards:

Green Card: I'm feeling great! I wish to be actively involved with everybody.

Blue Card: Overall, I'm doing OK. Feeling just a bit down.

Yellow Card: I'm having a "so-so" day. I may be a little touchy or moody so please leave me alone if I ask.

Orange Card: I'm either not feeling well or I'm upset with someone or something so please leave me alone until I change back to a different color card.
(Lisa must still interact with the teacher.)

Red Card: Lisa and other students are never allowed to use this card without permission from the teacher. A red card means that not only must the students leave Lisa alone; she is also exempt from interacting with the teacher and may be temporarily exempt from doing schoolwork.

STRATEGY #22
Congratulations! You're a Hall-Star

Many students have a problem with transition. They may behave fairly well in class but, when they get in the hall on the way to the cafeteria, look out! I usually keep a few HALL-STAR coupons in my pocket (see page 34). If I spot Jenny walking appropriately in the hall, I may give her a coupon and she becomes a HALL-STAR. At a later time, she can bring her coupon to my office for a star shaped lollipop. You'll be surprised how effective this strategy works during transition time.

STRATEGY #23
The Breathing Bell

Throughout the school day, you and your students need to take a few deep breaths. Set a timer to go off at random times. When the bell or buzzer goes off, everyone is to take three deep breaths and then return to work. Deep breathing relieves stress and stimulates brain cells.

STRATEGY # 24
Stubby Pencils and Pink Paper

Do you often get very frustrated with students who constantly come to class without certain supplies like pencils and paper? Try these tricks.

Keep a tin can on your desk. Encourage all students to find or bring used, short/stubby pencils to put in the tin can. For every donation they bring, they can have a piece of candy from your candy jar. You'll be amazed how full your tin will get. Now, whenever a student says, "I don't have a pencil," just tell him, "Help yourself to the tin."

For those students who don't bring paper, try this. Keep a stack of pink colored paper at your desk. When Josh says he has no paper, give him a piece of pink paper. As a class rule, all class work turned in on pink paper is an automatic five points off! Boys seem to really dislike this strategy. Note: Be sure to use your professional judgment here. Don't punish a child whose parents are unable to provide/afford paper.

STRATEGY #25
Reframing: A Different Way of Looking at Things

A few years ago I wrote a book called, *Every Child Has a Gift* (Youthlight, Inc.) which focused on my belief that every child was born with a certain gift, talent or strength. Even the worst behaved kid in class has a hidden talent. For example, the silly class clown may have a gift of humor. Instead of squelching his gift, how can we teach him to build positively on that strength? As educators we may want to look at some of our students negative characteristics in a different light. Let's do some reframing. Let's try to find some good in their bad habits. By looking at things in a positive way, we may help students realize that they do possess some hidden gifts/talents. Take a look at the list on page 35 for some reframing suggestions.

WAY TO GO!
You have been selected as a
HALL★STAR.

Take this coupon to _____ for a treat.

WAY TO GO!
You have been selected as a
HALL★STAR.

Take this coupon to _____ for a treat.

WAY TO GO!
You have been selected as a
HALL★STAR.

Take this coupon to _____ for a treat.

WAY TO GO!
You have been selected as a
HALL★STAR.

Take this coupon to _____ for a treat.

Positive Reframing

Characteristics/Behaviors	Reframing/Strengths
Bossiness	Leadership abilities
Slob	Laid back, casual, carefree
Silly	A potential stand-up comedian
Hyperactive	High energy, energetic
Nosey	Good news reporter
Strong-willed	Tenacious
Day dreamer	Creative, imaginative
Daring	Risk-taker
Lazy	Type B personality, laid back
Manipulator	Delegates to others to get the job done
Aggressive	Assertive
Questions authority	Independent, free thinker
Argumentative	Persuasive, future attorney
Poor hand-writer	Sign of a potential doctor
Always shouts out answers	Bet he/she does well on Jeopardy
Instigator	Initiator, innovative
Doodler/scribbler	Artistic abilities

STRATEGY #26
8 "Must Know" Facts about Children in Poverty

Do yourself and your students a big favor. Agree to attend a workshop or read a book that focuses on children living in poverty. Recently, I had the chance to hear Ruby K. Payne present her workshop, "A Framework for Understanding Poverty." What a rewarding, eye-opening experience! I now have much more patience and empathy for many of the children that I work with that live in poverty. I suggest checking out her website (www.ahaprocess.com) for upcoming workshops in your area.

What I learned from Ruby....

1. Low income parents show love for their children by buying things, mid-income parents show love by buying lessons.

2. In poverty, lighting is bad in homes and can affect a child's vision. Much dust in the house can affect health.

3. The noise level is higher in poor homes as the TV, stereo, or radio is always on. Then we wonder why some of these children are always loud in class!

4. In low-income homes, there is a wide range of behaviors that are considered acceptable.

5. A child's value in this group is based on his ability to entertain.

6. In these homes, parents often express/relate important messages non-verbally.

7. The education level of parents in these homes is low, which means children do not hear a lot of "words" and their vocabularies suffer.

8. Their poor nutrition slows learning and affects behavior.

STRATEGY #27
You Deserve a "Thumbs Up!"

In my desk I keep a supply of lollipops that are shaped like a thumb. Every once and a while, I'll surprise a student and give him one. I'll say to the student, "Jerry, I heard some good news about you. You deserve a "Thumbs Up!" I then give them the lollipop shaped like a thumb. The students get very excited about the treat and they also get a good feeling knowing that I am aware of the positive things they do.

STRATEGY #28
A Successful Pilot Needs a Good Co-Pilot

All schools today can benefit from an effective mentoring program. One of the best programs available today is, *The Co-Piloting Mentor Program* (bowman & bowman). It is an activity-based program in which "Co-Pilots" are mentors who help young people (the "Pilots") learn to take off and soar to new heights in their lives. The program includes a leader's guide and handbooks for mentors. The kit includes numerous hints, strategies, reproducibles, and other valuable information that will help you get a mentoring program started. For more information about "The Co-Piloting Mentor Program" check the website, www.youthlight.com.

STRATEGY #29
The Listening Skulls

Do you ever wish you had a dollar for every time you've used the word "listen?" I've tried numerous activities to help my students improve their listening skills. One of my most effective strategies involves my three plastic skulls that I keep in my office. At least once a year I carry my skulls to each class and tell the following story.

The Three Listening Skulls

Bahul was considered a "wise fool" throughout Baghdad. One day he sat in the marketplace with three skulls in front of him. In front of the first skull was a sign that said, "Free." In front of the second skull was a sign that read "One Cent." The third had a sign reading, "Priceless." All three skulls looked identical, and everyone who saw his booth was convinced that Bahul was crazy.

Finally, a man approached him and asked about the difference in prices. Bahul took a skewer (long, thin stick) and tried to put it through the ear hole of the first skull, but it would not go through. "See," he said, "nothing goes in. This skull isn't worth anything." He then tried the skewer on the second skull. It passed easily through both ear holes and slipped out on the other side. "You see, nothing stays in. What goes in one ear comes out the other. This skull is only worth a penny." When Bahul tried the third skull, the skewer passed easily through the first skull but not through the second. He said, "This skull is priceless. Whatever goes in, stays in."

While I tell the story, I demonstrate with my own plastic skulls and a stick. I then ask questions like: "Was Bahul really crazy or was he rather wise?" "Is your skull priceless?" "Has anyone ever told you that what goes in one ear comes out the other?" Throughout the year I mention the skull story often, especially when listening skills begin to slip.

STRATEGY #30
The "Must Avoid" Word

I once heard psychologist and parenting expert, John Rosemond tell of a conversation he had with a man on an airplane flight. The man told Rosemond that he owned a business with employees aged 25-60. He went on to say, "The work ethic of those above 40 is dramatically different from those below 30. Those above 40 know it's all about how they perform; their actions and behaviors. Those below 30 seem to think it's all about how they explain their behavior." I totally agree. It seems when students today do something wrong or do not get their work completed, they always seem to think they have valid excuses. Parents and teachers are often guilty of feeding this problem by asking, "Why?" Whenever we use the word "why," we're giving students an invitation to create a good reason or excuse for their action or lack of action. If you ask Joe, "Why did you hit Jake?" I'm sure he'll give you a good reason. If you see Jill throw a pencil and ask her "Why?" I'm sure she'll say something like, "Well, he threw it at me first."

I remember what Dr. William Glasser says to parents, "If you really love your children, you won't accept excuses." When we ask why, we're allowing children to come up with excuses. From now on, when you see Jasmine slap Vanna, don't ask why. Say, "Jasmine, I saw you slap her, go to the time-out area!" Children have to learn to take full responsibility for their actions.

STRATEGY #31
Individual Student Celebration Days

Think of a student you have had that caused many aggravating days and, because of his/her actions, had become alienated from the other students in the class. For instance, Jeremy is a student who constantly shouts out answers without raising his hand. His actions upset the teacher, and other students in class choose to ignore or tease him. There have been many days where the class got behind in their work or missed playtime because of Jeremy. This is turning into a stressful, tense situation. His teacher, Miss Willis has to do something.

She started keeping a chart on her desk noting the times that Jeremy shouted out responses. For three days in a row she noted improvement. On Thursday morning she told the class to stop working and listen for a special announcement. "Class, we have something special to celebrate. During the last few days Jeremy has been doing a much better job following certain class rules. Way to go Jeremy! Jeremy come to my desk and get a handful of "Homework Passes" and give one to everybody in class!"

This Individual Celebration Day let Jeremy know that the teacher had recognized his progress. That helped their relationship but, it also helped Jeremy with his peers because they all received a small reward because of his effort.

STRATEGY #32
Class Celebration Days

A class Celebration Day is a special, unannounced event or activity to recognize progress. For example, instead of telling your class on Monday morning, "If I have at least a 90% turn-in rating for homework in this class by Friday, we'll have a popcorn party," try this. Say, "Class, for the next few days I want you all to get caught up on your homework assignments." Don't hang any carrots in front of them. Then, let's assume that after a few days you notice an improvement. During class one day you announce, "Students please stop what you are doing, put your pencils down. Lately I've been very pleased with your efforts to get caught up on homework. Let's celebrate your progress by going outside for twenty minutes."

The goal here is to continue to get the students to be more responsible for their own work without always trying to earn a reward, privilege, or treat. Also, I have found that most classes look forward to these surprise events.

STRATEGY #33
Tick, Tick, Tick, Time is Wasting!

Teachers may want to consider keeping a stopwatch in their room. I'm talking about a large one that the students can see and one that makes a fairly loud ticking sound. Here are a few suggestions for using such an instrument.

- "Boys, you have three minutes to get in and out of the bathroom. If all of you aren't out in three minutes, I'm starting the clock and those added minutes will be deducted from playtime."

- "Tommy, this is the third time you left your book bag in the gym this week! Yes, you can go and get it, but as soon as you leave and until you return, the stopwatch will be ticking. If it takes you five minutes, you owe me five minutes after school time."

- "Class, it only took you three minutes to get ready. Great Job! Sue, drop two tokens in the jar."

- In his book, *Positive Classroom Discipline*, Fred Jones suggests using a stopwatch to decrease the number of disruptions. For instance, if two students are talking during the teacher's instruction time, he or she should stop the presentation, start the watch and say, "As soon as talking stops, then I'll stop this watch." The students know that minutes lost in instruction have to be made up and suggests taking those minutes lost from the fun activities that the students may enjoy doing on Fridays.

STRATEGY #34
Find a Niche and Scratch It!

I hope that you have found your niche in life and have found ample time to scratch it. But, what about your students? Have they found their niche? As teachers, we may need to help students find their niche and provide opportunities for them to scratch. Instead of always focusing on Cody's negative behaviors, recognize and focus on his strengths (i.e. sense of humor, artistic ability, helping others).

One of the best ways to help these students is to agree to coach a sport or head-up a club and invite them to join. If you aren't able to commit full-time to a club or a sport, try creating a specialized after school program that meets once a week or for a six to eight week block.

I remember a story in the very first edition of *Chicken Soup for the Soul* about a middle school teacher in Harlem, New York who created an after school chess club. Even though many of his colleagues didn't think his students were smart enough to learn chess, he went on with the club. His activity became overwhelmingly successful as numerous kids decided to stay after school and learn chess rather than roam the streets. So many of his kids began to excel that he took some of them to Russia to play the best in the world. His club saved many kids from ending up in trouble.

Every year at my school I direct a wrestling club. It seems that almost all my "behavior" students sign up. Many of the students get to participate for three years (grades 3-5). Thanks to the club, they learn discipline, skills, sportsmanship and many go on to successful wrestling careers at the high-school. I often tell others, "With some of the most difficult students I've worked with, I can honestly say that I was able to make more progress with them in a week of wrestling than I did in ten counseling sessions in my office."

Create your own club. Help students scratch their niches.

STRATEGY #35
When Mother Nature Calls

How would you like a class in which there is seldom a behavior problem, the students work well in groups, everyone does their homework, students don't want to leave when the bell rings, and every year the students beg the counselor to put them in your class. Is it possible? Yes, according to the author Sue Halpern. In her book, *Four Wings and a Prayer*, she introduces us to a high school Biology teacher named Terry Callender from Wamego, Kansas.

During the last few years, his students captured, measured, weighed, tagged and released thousands of Monarch butterflies. Thanks to Callender and his students, scientists have learned much about the habits of Monarchs. His kids just can't seem to get enough butterfly work and many days he has to force them to leave so they won't be late for the buses.

Terry Callender's butterfly project has enabled him to teach academics, social skills and character education in unique ways...

Math: Students have to weigh butterflies, count them, and estimate the number of miles they travel.

Weather: They studied wind conditions, cloud formation, and monitored temperatures.

Geography: They studied maps and routes that the butterflies travel through the United States and Mexico. His students found that the record for the longest distance traveled by one butterfly was 2,880 miles!

Science: Students had to be able to identify the gender of each butterfly. They also studied the aerodynamics of how they fly.

Social Skills: Students learned how to work in groups, to be patient, to brainstorm and how to be receptive to other people's ideas.

Character Education: By helping butterflies, students learned about compassion.

Students need to get outside and learn lessons from animals and nature. Following are three handouts to use with your students.

 **Animal Guardian Angels:** Students agree to select an animal that they will assist and then develop a plan to prove that they are helping (see page 42). Myself, I am a guardian angel for turtles. Whenever I see one trying to cross the road, I stop my car, get out, and carry the turtle to the other side.

 Tikkun Club: Tikkun is a Hebrew word that is often translated as "world repair." Start a Tikkun Club in your room or school. Students will sign a contract and list things that they will do to make the world a better place. The students can decide to recycle, not litter, feed birds, not waste water, and volunteer to do things to protect the environment. (see page 43)

 Mallard Marathon: This is a neat activity to educate your students about ducks and culminates with a plastic, toy duck race in the river. The students will go "bonkers" over this event. (see page 44)

I believe that when students learn to be kind, compassionate and caring about our environment and animals, they tend to be better human beings. Mother Nature is calling our kids.

Animal Guardian Angels

"If you have men who will exclude any of God's creatures from the shelter of compassion and pity, you will have men who will deal likewise with their fellow man." — *Saint Francis of Assisi*

"Until he extends the circle of compassion to all living things, man will not himself find peace." — *Albert Schweitzer*

I, _____, agree with the words of these two men, Saint Francis of Assisi and Albert Schweitzer. I agree to show compassion to all animals.

As of this date, _____, I will become a Guardian Angel for _____ (select an animal).

To show compassion for the above stated animal, I promise to:

1.

2.

3.

4.

5.

Student Signature_____

Teacher Signature_____

Tikkun Club

Tikkun is a Hebrew word that is often translated as "world repair."

I, _____, as a member of my school's Tikkun Club agree to do the following things to, not only repair our world, but to make it a better place for those who follow in the future. I understand the importance of caring for the environment and our animals.

My Plan:

_____

_____

_____

_____

_____

_____

_____

_____

_____

_____

Student Signature _____

Teacher/Club Leader Signature _____

Date: _____

"The goal in life is living in agreement with nature."
– *Zeno, Greek Philosopher (490-430 BC)*

Mallard Marathon

PURPOSE:
1. To increase students' awareness of the many species of ducks in the United States. To learn more about their habits, migration routes, diet, and mating/nesting.
2. To learn how the word "duck" has become part of our language and how it is used in many animal expressions.
3. To discover ways to show compassion for this animal.

MATERIALS:
1. A guide of The Sibley Guide to Birds or other books that show different species of ducks. Access to encyclopedias.
2. Plastic weighted ducks. Up to three per student.
3. Permanent black marker.

CLASS LESSONS:
1. Have each student do a report on one specie of duck that includes where it lives, migration routes, color, nesting and eating habits.
2. Have group discussions on how we can show compassion to ducks.
3. If possible, travel to a park, pond, or river to view them.
4. Ask students what the following expressions mean:
   • like water off a duck's back
   • the ugly duckling
   • lame duck
   • if it walks like a duck, quacks like a duck, it's probably a duck

THE MALLARD MARATHON:
1. At the end of the unit, schedule a Mallard Marathon.
2. Based on how well the students participated in the unit, they can earn up to three plastic weighted ducks. Be sure each student earns at least one. Students will use permanent markers to identify their ducks. Have the students use numbers as identification.
3. Make arrangements with your local Parks and Recreation Department or county government to allow your students to race their ducks in a river or stream.
4. Schedule time, date, and location. Arrange for transportation. Have parents sign field trip participation forms.
5. Have a starting point for students to drop their ducks in the water. Have a finish line at least a mile away. The ducks are to float unassisted down stream.
6. Transport students to finish line.
7. Have parent volunteers to help ducks that get stuck.
8. Just for the fun of it, have a few small prizes for: first place, second, third, middle of the pack, and the last place duck.
9. Finish the trip with a picnic in nature.
10. Make this a yearly trip for your class.

STRATEGY #36
A Good Behavior Booster Shot

Do you want to see a quick, positive change in the behavior of some of your more challenging students? Start giving your students a grade in creativity. See if you can add a new column to report cards in order to add each student's grade in "Creativity." So many of our children are graded/evaluated solely on their analytical abilities but, many of these same youngsters are very creative. Acknowledge this special talent. On a writing project, you might give Aaron a D for his writing skills but an A for his creativity. In his book, *Successful Intelligence*, Robert Sternberg tells of his experience as a teacher who rewarded creativity. "I explicitly reward creative efforts among my students. For example, when I assign papers, I tell them that I will look for the usual skills – namely, a demonstration of knowledge, their display of analytical skills, and, of course, good writing. But above and beyond that, I look for and reward creativity." (p. 211). Getting a good grade in creativity may be the "booster shot" that some kids need.

STRATEGY #37
A Friend in Need

I encourage teachers to find time to get to know the school's Occupational Therapist well. A well-trained O.T. has a keen eye and can often see things in children that most of us might miss. Let me give you a personal story. A fourth grade boy named Jeremy was referred to me because of his negative attitude and anger problems. After four or five counseling sessions I saw little progress. Then, one day the Occupational Therapist visited Jeremy's class to observe another student. Later that day, she asked me if I knew a fourth grade boy named Jeremy. I shared my experience with the boy and also told of my frustrations by the lack of progress. The O.T., based on a short observation, believed she found one of the causes of his anger. She said, "Tom, Jeremy grabs his pencil so hard when writing you can see the ends of his fingers getting white. He also places too much of his weight over the top of his desk and he lacks some important fine motor skills. Writing is a painful, difficult task for him. No wonder he gets upset and refuses to work."

We signed the referral forms with his parents and he started visiting the O.T. After only a few sessions with her he was able to sit properly, hold the pencil better, and was more relaxed. His anger outbursts decreased dramatically.

When you encounter a challenging student, seek help from others in the school. I've made our school's O.T. one of my "buddies."

STRATEGY #38
Quiet is Not Always "F.I.N.E."

Have you ever had a student, family member or co-worker who used the word "fine" almost every time you ask them how they were doing? I've heard the word "fine" is an acronym for: Feelings Inside Never Expressed. At times I tend to get concerned with students who are always quiet and who always respond to questions with one word answers such as yes, no, and fine. Some of these passive students may have a laid back, calm temperament. However, you should make valid attempts to get them to open up more during conversations. Provide a safe, non-threatening environment. Be observant. Watch them with their peers. Do they laugh, talk and play? Could they be the victims of teasing/bullying? Could they be having family problems? We tend to devote so much of our time and energy on disruptive students, but lets not overlook the quiet ones. So often, when you hear about a student who commits suicide or enters the school with a gun, his teachers respond by saying, "I never expected him to do something like that. He was always so quiet and well-behaved."

STRATEGY #39
Drumsticks, Squeeze Balls, and Pens

Have you attended a rock and roll concert in which, at the end of the show, the drummer threw his sticks into the crowd? Then did you notice how the rabid fans fought to get one of those sticks? Now, we may not be rock and roll stars, and we may not have a lot of rabid fans (students) but, I still believe that most students look up to and respect us. They also enjoy receiving a personal item of ours and that exchange can help us develop closer relationships.

I usually keep a good supply of stress/squeeze balls in my office. Throughout each week, students see me carrying, squeezing or tossing the yellow balls. Then sometime on Friday afternoons, I give the ball to a student. It's amazing how excited they get. I love hearing, "Hey, Mr. Carr gave me his ball!"

If you aren't into squeeze balls, try this. Have some personalized pens made. On each pen you can have your name, a favorite quote or a study skill. Make sure the pens are unique in color and design. At the end of each week or at the end of the day, give someone the pen you have been using. I think the kids will enjoy getting the pen that you used rather than just taking one out of the box. You'll be pleasantly pleased with all the good things that happen once you distribute your pens.

Suggestions:

- Quietly hand the pen to the child. Don't make a big show of it, otherwise you may see signs of jealousy or anger.

- Keep tract of the kids you give pens to, so that you'll be able to make sure almost everyone gets one.

- Give them away with no strings attached. Don't say. "I'll give the pen to the student who scores the highest on today's quiz."

- Early in the school year you may want to give your pens to those students who appear rather challenging. It may help you "connect" with them quicker.

STRATEGY #40
The 98% Guarantee for Parents

There's an old saying that goes, "The friends you keep, determines the trouble you meet." I believe there is a lot of truth to that statement. Parents need to be constantly aware of with whom their children are spending their free time. Parents can coach or navigate their children toward positive peers by keeping them busy in positive activities such as sports, church, scouts, and other organized programs. Over the years, I've noticed that the students who are actively engaged in beneficial after-school activities tend to graduate from high school. Students who do not get involved often do not graduate.

I devised a point system called my 98% Guarantee (see page 48). If a child, by middle school, scores at least a two out of seven points on the score sheet, then I believe he or she has about a 98% chance of graduating from high school and staying out of major trouble. Share a copy of the 98% Guarantee Score Sheet with your parents. Also, mention to them the following six points.

- Parents might need to cut back a little on chores so children will have time for homework and extra time to be involved in after school activities.

- Quite often, parents will feel like a taxi cab driver as they transport their children back and forth to practice, church, etc.

- Parents should not force children into activities. Instead, they may want to "prime the pump" by inviting children to join and by exposing them to other children who are actively involved in sports, clubs, etc.

- When children are involved, parents need to be there to support them.

- If Alvin's grades drop in school, don't make him quit Little League Baseball. Instead, take away some of his privileges or take him to see a tutor.

- Start getting kids involved at a young age. Once Lindsay gets to middle school it will be almost impossible to get her involved. Once kids get "hooked" into a positive peer group at a young age, they tend to want to stay in that group. If children don't fit into a positive group of peers early on they tend to seek out more negative friends.

©2003 YouthLight, Inc.

The 98% Guarantee
Score Sheet for Parents

By middle school your child should score a minimum of two points on this scale. A good average is three or four. Children who score a six or a seven may be too busy. They can get burn-out and may not have enough family time. Children scoring a zero or a one may be headed for trouble.

____ 1. Child gets one point for each full-time, organized sport at school. Team must practice regularly and have a coach. Examples include football, baseball, softball, volleyball, wrestling, soccer, track, cross country, golf, tennis, etc.

____ 2. Child gets one point for each of the following outside of school sports/activities. Once again, these programs must be organized with a practice schedule, leader, etc. Gymnastics, martial arts, dance, swimming, youth recreational sports, etc.

____ 3. One point for being actively involved with a church, temple, synagogue or other religious groups. Child could be in youth group, choir, etc. and attend services almost every week.

____ 4. One point if actively involved in one or more of these musical areas; band, chorus, piano or other instrumental lessons, singing etc.

____ 5. One point for serious volunteer work. This means spending a minimum of five hours a week helping others in the community.

____ 6. One point for being actively involved in scouts, 4-H, and other adult-lead organizations.

____ 7. One point for being actively involved in one or more of the following hobbies/interests. Must devote a minimum of five hours a week. Art, writing, drawing, poetry, sports card collecting, hiking, jogging, climbing, stamp or rock collecting, model planes, horseback riding, and other similar activities.

____ **TOTAL POINTS**

STRATEGY #41
Caution! Inappropriate Praise At Work

Praise, if used properly can be very effective. Just the opposite is true; too much praise or praise used inappropriately can backfire. New teachers are trained to believe that they need to give out much praise to help encourage or motivate students. In some schools, teachers are evaluated on the amount of praise they use. Also, it seems that whenever teachers consult with a behavior expert about difficult students, the "expert" usually asks, "Are you praising him/her often?" Praise is not the answer to all problems. In fact, I've noticed that some of the best teachers I've observed do not use a lot of praise, and when they use it, they are very selective.

Here are some thoughts on the use of praise:

- Too much praise becomes phony. Children recognize phony praise!

- Praise often sets up competition in the classroom. For instance, if you say, "Mary, way to go! You are the only one in class that followed instructions exactly as told. You get an extra ten minutes free time," Imagine how some of the other students will react? Will there be jealousy or anger in the room?

- Too much praise limits creativity. Studies have shown that when students receive a lot of praise they reach a point where they will not do extra work, take risks, or try harder work because if they are unsuccessful, they believe they won't get the praise they desire.

- Be especially careful using praise with students who have Oppositional Defiant Disorder. These children do not like to be controlled or manipulated by people in positions of authority. If you praise them, especially in front of their peers, their behavior may actually get worse.

- When you praise, be specific. Don't say, "You are a great artist," say, "I like the choice of colors you used in the background."

- Do not always praise results, praise effort. "Kelly, I like the way you really worked hard on that problem."

- Reverse the praise. Instead of saying, "Willie, I'm so proud of you. You got a 95 on your Science test," say, "Willie, you must be so proud of yourself for doing so well on your test."

STRATEGY #42
The Wandering Tattler

Got a problem with tattling in your class? Let the Wandering Tattler help you. Follow these three steps carefully and you'll see much improvement.

1. **Tell them about this fascinating bird.** The Wandering Tattler is a shorebird that summers in Alaska and northwest Canada and winters on the coasts from California to Australia. It is a solitary bird that is seldom seen in groups. It got its name from its annoying, shrieking sounds. The hunters don't like the bird because its call scares away all the other birds. It seems as though this bird is tattling on the hunters. Often the hunter will try to shoot the Wandering Tattler first. The bird seems to wander endlessly, and when frightened, will crouch and hide instead of flying away. Although this bird is nowhere near extinction, its numbers are decreasing.

2. **Compare this bird to students who tattle.** Students who like to tell on others share many of the same characteristics of this bird. They like to wander around and get in other peoples business, they are so annoying that they become solitary (no one wants to be their friends) and they tend to run and hide when others come looking for them.

3. **Explain the Wandering Tattler Form** (see next page). Make sure your students know the difference between tattling and reporting important information. Tell your students that you do not take verbal tattles. If they wish to tell on someone, they must fill out the Wandering Tattler form and drop it in the box. My experience has found that once students realize that they must write their concern on a form, tattling quickly decreases.

STRATEGY #43
Get Out the Masking Tape

Have you ever had a student who never seems to be able to keep his/her mouth closed for even a minute or two? Let's say that you have to teach a very important lesson to your class but you know that your very talkative student, Lindy, probably won't cooperate. Try this: "Lindy, I need you to follow the class rules concerning talking while I teach the next lesson. I don't have the time to keep stopping to ask you to be quiet. I'm placing these five pieces of masking tape on your desk. Every time you talk out of turn I will remove a piece of tape. If I have to remove the last piece before this lesson is over, then I'm calling your parents this evening."

Many students are visual in their learning. By letting them see the pieces of tape being removed, it helps as a reminder. Also, I notice how well some of the talkative students can control themselves once they get down to the last piece of masking tape!

The Wandering Tattler Form

Dear _____,   Date_____

I need to tell you…

_____

_____

_____

_____

_____

_____

Before dropping this form in the box, be sure to check your spelling, grammar, punctuation, and capitalization. Do you have an introductory sentence and a good closing sentence?

The Wandering Tattler Form

Dear _____,   Date_____

I need to tell you…

_____

_____

_____

_____

_____

_____

Before dropping this form in the box, be sure to check your spelling, grammar, punctuation, and capitalization. Do you have an introductory sentence and a good closing sentence?

STRATEGY #44
Dumping the Whole Bucket

When a student gets upset and begins to vent, one of the best things you can do is to let angry student "dump the whole bucket" before you say anything. While the student is venting, don't interrupt. When the student appears to be finished say, "I have listened and now I want to write down a few things so I am sure I have all of this straight. Would you please tell me again what you've just told me?" By letting the student dump the whole bucket while you listen and then by asking them to repeat their concerns, they tend to calm down quickly.

STRATEGY #45
The "No Discount Contract"

Have your class develop and sign a "No Discount Contract." This is an agreement between class members to avoid discounting, cutting down, putting down, and ratting (Tongue Fu Artistry) each other in hurtful ways. By signing, they agree to not tease, bully, or make inappropriate racial and gender comments. Each student also agrees to not put him/herself down. (see next page)

STRATEGY #46
The Deceptive Book Exchange

I heard of a clever idea that two teachers used to help them deal with a disruptive student. Teacher A had a boy in her class that often got out of hand and needed to leave the room for a while. She felt that the boy did not need to go to the office. He just lacked self-control and was rather impulsive but, he was capable of getting his act together if he was allowed to leave class for a short period of time. Whenever the boy needed to be removed, the teacher would hand him a book and tell him to take it to Teacher B. Depending on the size of the book, Teacher B knew how long to keep him. If the boy carried a small book, then Teacher B kept him for five minutes. If the boy brought a large book, then Teacher B knew Teacher A needed a longer break.

NO DISCOUNT
CONTRACT

As members of this class we agree
to treat each other in positive ways.

We agree not to:

- Tease
- Bully
- Make fun of others
- Use inappropriate racial or gender comments

We also agree not to put ourselves down.

Student Signatures…

Witnesses:

*Date:*_____

STRATEGY #47
The Worry Wall

Somewhere in your room keep a small corkboard on the wall. Call this area your Worry Wall. Throughout the year, if you begin to have worries or concerns about class behaviors (i.e., teasing, lying, stealing) or academic issues (i.e., homework problems, poor test scores) share them with your students. Then ask for suggestions on how things can be changed or improved. Tell them to write their thoughts on a specially provided form and attach it to the Worry Wall. Students do not have to write their names on the form. You'll be amazed by the many neat ideas kids will come up with that will help improve things.

STRATEGY #48
Walk That Walk

Is teasing and/or bulling a problem in your class or school? If it is, then let's get some suggestions from a "mugger."

A few years ago I saw a mugger being interviewed on television. A psychologist asked the man in prison, "How did you pick your victims? How could you tell which people were safe to attack?" The man replied, "I never picked my victims based on their size, age, gender, or what they were wearing." He continued, "I knew who to grab based on how they walked." He went into more detail as follows:

Fast walkers: The man noted that these people were good targets because he felt that they were afraid or nervous. Also, fast walkers seldom looked around to check their surroundings.

Slow walkers with head down: The man noted that muggers went after these types of individuals for two reasons. Once again, these people, just like the fast walkers, rarely checked out what was going on around them. Secondly, when people walked this way it could mean that they were sad, worried, had low self-esteem, and were not very assertive. These walkers were often attacked.

Steady-paced, heads up walkers: Muggers usually didn't bother these people. They appear secure, confident, unafraid, and very observant.

If muggers pick their victims by the way they walk, then is it possible that teasers and bullies pick their victims by how they carry themselves? I always remember my father telling me, "Keep your head up and walk like you like yourself!"

Find time to talk to your students about the way they carry themselves and how they walk. Do some role-playing, practice walking, and encourage your students to walk "tall." These activities should eliminate some of these teasing and bullying in school.

STRATEGY #49
Nice Police... Mean Police

This strategy provides parents and teachers with a clever approach for helping children become more responsible for their behavior. (see page 56)

STRATEGY #50
The Peace Rug™

Here is a neat program to teach children how to resolve conflicts in a non-violent way. Supply your classroom with a Peace Rug™. It is a beautiful rug that features a serene cloud design. The rug is kept rolled up in the corner of the room and when two students are having problems getting along they are encouraged to unroll the rug, sit on it, and begin to discuss concerns. The developers of this unique idea report, "Schools have found the Peace Rug™ to be a simple concept and successful tool to teach all grade levels. Moreover, this one program contains all the elements for state-mandated curriculum instruction in the areas of conflict resolution, anger management, communication skills, interpersonal skills, character education, and bully-victim violence prevention. It also helps with cultural diversity issues." For more information go to: www.peacerug.com.

STRATEGY #51
The Stationary Bicycle

Look in your closet. Go to a yard sale. Stop by your local used sporting goods store. I'm sure you'll find an inexpensive stationary bicycle to put in your classroom. Who cares if others think it's weird having such an item in class. On rainy days or when Hank gets fidgety, let him get on the bike and peddle for a few minutes. Be sure to put a stand or rack on the handlebars so he can place his reading book there while peddling. We don't want him to get behind in his work. Make the bike available to all students.

COLOR CODE YELLOW

Nice Police...Mean Police*

Objective: This activity encourages students to take more responsibility for their actions. Students will be able to accept consequences given to them by teachers without the teacher having to do a lot of yelling, lecturing, or threatening. This strategy is aimed at helping students and teachers do less talking and take more action.

Setting the Stage: Ask the student, "Which of these two police officers would you rather have pull you over if you were driving your car too fast?"

- *"Nice Police Officer"* who is polite and quickly writes up your ticket. He/she does not lecture you and ends by saying, "Drive carefully and have a nice day."

- *"Mean Police Officer,"* who does a lot of yelling and is very rude. He/she says, "What is wrong with you? You know the law. Where did you get your license, in a cereal box?" The officer continues, "You better straighten up or you'll end up in jail. I hope I never see you around here again."

Taking Action: Tell the student you will do your best to act like the Nice Police Officer. Whenever the student breaks a major class rule you will calmly and politely write him/her a ticket. You will not lecture or be rude. You will also try to be the type of officer who writes "reward tickets" when you spot a student doing something good.

Ticket issued to: _____ Date: _____

Violation: _____

_____

Consequence: _____

Signature of Officer: _____

Reward ticket issued for: _____ Date: _____

Ticket received for: _____

_____

Reward: _____

Signature of Officer: _____

*Adapted from, "Good Cops and Bad Cops in Parenting" by Lorna L. Hecker in The Therapist's Notebook, Hecker, Lorna and Deacon, Shanon. Harworth Press, New York 1998

STRATEGY #52
Announcing the Appointment of Class Experts

Sometime during the second or third month of the school year try this neat idea with your class (third grade and up). Gather them together and say, "Let me tell you a quick story about an amazing man."

Thomas Fuller was a slave who lived in Virginia in the late 1700's. Although he could not read or write, he was pretty good at arithmetic. One day a friend of his, Dr. Benjamin Rush, decided to ask Thomas Fuller a tough question to see how good he was with counting. The doctor asked him, "How many seconds would a man have lived if he was alive for 70 years, 17 days, and 12 hours?" After a minute and a half, Thomas said, "2,210,500,800 seconds." The doctor then replied, "Thomas, your calculation is off a bit." The slave then said, "But massa, you forgot the leap years."

Then tell the class, "After reading that story I realized that even though the slave couldn't read or write, he was an expert in math. Then I realized that almost everybody is an expert in something. There are many experts in this class. Max, you're an expert on NASCAR. Laurie, you're a great poet. Hank, I've never seen anyone kick a ball as far as you. If I need help identifying insects, all I have to do is ask Heather for help. All of us in here know who to go to if we need tasty brownies for a party... Seth! I feel lucky to be surrounded by experts."

Then tell the students that you have an important announcement. Unroll an old-looking scroll, blow a horn or trumpet and read, "As of this date (state the date) I officially appoint everyone in here a "Class Expert." I now will give each of you your official certificate of appointment (see next page). On the certificate you will note your area of expertise and you will promise to constantly update your skills by reading and researching to learn even more. As an expert, you agree to;
1) Provide me and others in the class with information about your expertise,
2) You will make valid attempts to find the correct information if you do not know the answer. As a teacher, I will refer to you as, "Doctor" when I seek your assistance in a specialized area."

CLASS EXPERT
Certificate of Appointment

Let it be known that of this date _____,

_____ (name of student) is considered to

be an expert on the topic of _____.

The appointed student realizes that by being an expert, he/she must...

- Be willing to share his/her expertise with teacher and students
- Do the best to search for the answers to questions he/she doesn't know about his/her area of expertise
- Continually research and update skills
- Not be boastful

Student Signature _____

Teacher Signature _____

Let it also be known that the holder of this certificate will be addressed as "Doctor" by the teacher when asked questions about his/her area of expertise.

STRATEGY #53
Sports Talk 101

Sports bring people together. When strangers meet they either talk about the weather or sports. Have you ever noticed how often adults use sports metaphors in their day to day conversations? I believe that by using sports terms/language with some of our more difficult students (especially boys) we may form better relationships. A lot of students play baseball, softball, and basketball and are quite familiar with the rules and terms used during games. Why not use basketball slang or metaphors when correcting a defiant boy like Lenny? How about using sports talk when helping Karen who is an all-star softball player? Brush up on your sports; it could benefit your classroom. Here are a few baseball terms that might help you get started:

7th inning stretch: time to take a break

There's two outs in the bottom of the ninth: time is running out

No hits, no runs, no errors: perfect

Three strikes and you're out: you only get three chances

Foul ball: a rude statement or a comment that was inappropriate

Bring in the relief pitcher: we need help

Double-header: two tests on the same day

You threw me a curveball: you surprised me

You need some more pine tar: because you keep dropping things

You're in the ballpark: your answer is close

STRATEGY #54
Avoid Punishing Students for Their Weaknesses

All students possess strengths and weaknesses. Sure, they need to work on their deficiencies, but should they be punished by withholding them from activities that allow them to shine, while they work on their deficiencies? In his book, *A Mind at a Time*, Dr. Mel Levine states, "Equally cruel is the practice of punishing a kid for his weakness while banning the use of his strengths." (p. 319).

Ponder the following questions:

- Jake is a fantastic artist and loves going to Mrs. Parker's Art class on Tuesdays but he struggles with his handwriting. Should he be held out of Art to work on his handwriting?

- For some reason, Heather is poor in spelling. She is the best kickball player in the fourth grade. Is it right to say, "Heather, you can't play kickball today because you need to practice your spelling."?

- Tameka is very creative in her science class. She often produces the most amazing inventions. Her teacher tells her one day, "No more science for you this week, you have to spend more time at learning long division." Is that fair?

Help kids with their weaknesses but don't punish them through their strengths. Instead of kicking Juwan off the basketball team for poor grades, get him a tutor. Most kids, like Juwan, who get put off the team don't usually spend their extra time in the library; they'll spend it in the streets.

STRATEGY #55
"Class, Was There Something Else I Could've Done?"

Frustration often sets in when you've tried everything with a child and nothing seems to work. Then one day you finally have to tell that student to leave the room or go to the office. As soon as the student leaves, call a time-out and ask your class, "Was there something else I could've done differently with Ellen?" By asking this question, it sends the message that you really care about Ellen and that you really didn't want to have her removed. Also, by asking this question, you are opening the door for suggestions/ways of helping Ellen. Many times your students will provide new insights and possible solutions that you haven't thought of using.

This strategy is not a sign of weakness. In fact, you will probably gain even more respect from your students. Never be afraid to seek input from students.

STRATEGY #56
I'll Take Two Dozen Floating Key-chains Please!

Do you have a restless group of students who cannot seem to sit quietly and keep their hands to themselves? Go to the sporting goods store and purchase a set of floating key-chains, one for every student. Most floating key-chains are brightly colored, made of foam rubber that can be squeezed like a stress ball, and usually have a little chain so students can attach them to belt loops or book-bags. Here are a few strategies for implementing this strategy.

- Each student is given one. Let them know the key-chain belongs to you, must be kept in the room, but at the end of the year each student gets to take theirs home.

- Students are told to keep their key-chains close by. Whenever they get angry, frustrated, or a bit restless, they are to squeeze them five times. When the Breathing Bell rings (see strategy #23) they are to squeeze their key-chains.

- Students are informed that if they have a concern with another student they are to squeeze their key-chains five times before talking to him/her.

- With a marker, number each key-chain then put a corresponding number of tickets in a hat. Just for fun, have an occasional drawing for goodies or extra privileges. If a student's number is picked from the hat, he or she is a winner if he/she has his/her key-chain.

- Teach the students other strategies on using their key-chains to help them, relax, control anger, and burn off energy by squeezing often throughout the day.

STRATEGY #57
Running Leads to Calming

In my book, *Every Child Has a Gift*, I tell of a psychologist named Tom Scott who works with children who have Attention Deficit Disorder and Attention Deficit/Hyperactivity Disorder. He has had much success with these children by introducing them to the form of play we call running. Scott himself suffered from ADHD while growing up. Scott said, "school was never easy for me because my ADHD went undiagnosed until after college. I was impulsive, distracted, had low self-esteem, and a huge overflow of energy. I spent a lot of time in the hall." He still remembers a second grade teacher who once stuck masking tape over his mouth and stood him in front of the class for over an hour. Somehow he made it to college and while running twice a day for the track team he realized that he retained information much better in the hour or two after his workouts.

If you find yourself with several active, hyper, and high energy students, consider running as a positive outlet. If you aren't a runner, find a faculty member or someone in the community who is, and start a running club. Encourage the students to run laps before school starts each day. If possible, give them opportunities to run after school as well. You'll soon find that running actually helps calm most children.

STRATEGY #58
Know When It's Time to Wave the White Flag

Many of our adolescents aren't great in math or reading but, they are experts in arguing. As teachers, we know it's almost impossible to win an argument with an angry student. In fact, I've heard that there has never been an incident, anywhere in the world, where an adult got in the last word with an adolescent! Even if we think we get the last word, upset students find ways to get back at us (i.e. giving us an obscene gesture when we turn our back, vandalizing the boy's room, or sabotaging our next math lesson). They use these negative actions to "get the last word." Consider some of the following strategies for dealing with the argumentative student.

- Know when it is time to stop playing volleyball with the student. No matter what you say, the student will say something in return.

- When it gets "heated," remove *yourself* rather than asking the student to leave.

- Remember, when you and a student argue, it becomes a power struggle. Do not put yourself in a no-win situation by saying something like, "I don't want to hear another word out of you!"

- If you are in a difficult situation where you can't remove yourself and where other students are watching you and the angry student, try this. Say to the student, "William, I've said all I want to on this discussion. I'm giving you permission to get in the last word. Go ahead and say what you want." By giving the student permission to get in the last word, you remain in control. William might think he won the battle but, don't forget that you granted him permission to get in the last word.

- Remember to save your energy with this type of student. Concede and wave the white flag. Wait until the dust settles before you and the student open up a positive line of communication.

STRATEGY #59
Beware the Revenge Factor

According to research completed by Lochman, Whidby and FitzGerald (2000), chronically aggressive boys often place high value on revenge behavior. For some boys, not to seek revenge is a sign of weakness. Many have been told by their parents, "Be a man and hit back!" So let's say that you saw Mark hit Luis and you intervened and praised Luis for not hitting back. In your mind you are praising Luis and believe that it will help him to learn how to resolve conflict without violence. However, Luis does not want this type of praise. He doesn't want to "just forget about it" because he believes that forgetting about it is bad. In a way Luis is saying, "Why am I getting praise for something that is bad?" So, instead of praising him, stay neutral and say something like, "Luis, let's go for a walk and reflect on what just happened."

STRATEGY #60
Encouraging Parents to "Work the System"

At one time or another, most children will encounter academic problems in school. In his book, *Beyond the Classroom*, Laurence Steinberg compared the ways parents of successful students and parents of unsuccessful students handled problems.

Steinberg found, "Parents of unsuccessful students try to handle the problem themselves, at home. They increase their vigilance over their child's homework, offer to help with assignments, implement more demanding study schedules for the child to follow after school and on weekends, and so on. When this fails, as it typically does, the parents often feel frustrated and get angry at their child. Schoolwork then becomes an area of contention in the household, which only interferes with the child's chances of improving." (p. 127).

Parents of successful students, in contrast, mobilize the school on their child's behalf – they "work the system." Provide your parents with a copy of How to Work the System.

HOW TO WORK THE SYSTEM*

Parents, if your child begins to do poorly in school, don't always try to solve the problem at home. Go on the offence. Contact the school and learn how to "work the system."

- Become a familiar face at school. Go to meetings, attend special events, conference with the teacher on a regular basis. Get to know the principal, counselor, and other support personnel. Don't be the type of parent that only shows up when there's a problem.

- If your daughter is having a problem in math, don't try to resolve the problem by having her do more math. It is useful to realize that most parents seldom have the experience or knowledge to assist their children with academic difficulties.

- Contact the school and schedule a meeting with the teacher.

- If things do not improve, schedule another meeting. This time involve the principal and the counselor.

- By meeting with school personnel, it sends a strong message to the child. It shows that the parent has faith in the school's ability to help.

- If the school suggests certain home exercises that require your participation, be sure to cooperate.

- If the school agrees to implement new strategies to help your child, check back in a week or two to make sure they are following through with their agreement.

- If necessary, be assertive but be patient as well. "As in dealing with any organization, squeaky wheels get the grease."

*Adapted from, *Beyond the Classroom*, by Laurence Steinberg, Simon & Schuster, New York, 1996.

COLOR CODE YELLOW

STRATEGY #61
Soothing Stones

According to Webster's Dictionary, the word "soothe" means, "to calm, comfort, compose, tranquilize; to relieve (pain etc.)." So many of our difficult students can benefit from things that soothe them. Keep a small jar of "soothing stones" hidden in the bottom drawer of your desk. In the jar you should have several small stones that are smooth-surfaced and lightly colored (light blue, gray, white). When you have a student that has trouble controlling his anger, is easily upset, or is dealing with pain, invite him to select a smooth stone from your jar. Keep this exchange discreet; it is a special interaction between you and the student. Encourage the student to keep the stone in his pocket and to use it as follows:

- When things get hectic and you feel you're loosing control, notice and feel the smoothness of the stone. It will remind you that things in your life will eventually be smooth again.

- When angry, rub the stone with a lot of pressure. Rub the anger into the stone.

- When feeling pain, rub your pain into the stone.

- Notice the stone's hardness, toughness. Remember that you can be tough and face adversities that occur in life.

- When you get nervous or restless, toss, jiggle, play with the stone.

- Find time to closely study your stone. Notice the colors, the texture, the small specks and designs. Just like you, it is a beautiful thing that was created for this world. Make the most of your life!

STRATEGY #62
Special Delivery

Many of our most difficult students appear to be self-centered. All they care about is themselves. Seldom do they help others and seldom do they show empathy or compassion. They also seem more interested in receiving than in giving. Here is a strategy that has proven helpful in changing the attitudes of some of these students. Appoint them as your special delivery person. Have Johnny take a tray of cookies to the office for the hard working secretaries. Tori can be asked to take a small gift to the janitor on his birthday. When your class makes thank-you notes for the cafeteria workers, get Jeremy to make the delivery. Have Lilly deliver the welcome basket to the new fifth grader. Quite often, these "hard-core" students come back with a new attitude as they had a chance to witness the power of giving.

STRATEGY #63
25 + 25 = AHA!

I've never been one who approves of students writing sentences as a form of punishment. I have a different approach to the use of writing when it comes to discipline. If a student misbehaves or if he wishes to earn back some privileges, he should have the option of writing/copying some of the AHA! Quotes (see next page). Either you or the student should select one of the quotes. Also, you may wish to put the quotes in a bag and draw them out at random. The student then writes the positive quote 25 times. The student has the option of reading the quote privately to you or out loud to the class. The belief is that if he writes the quote 25 times and reads the quote 25 times, it may begin to register in his mind. He might go, "AHA! I never thought of that!"

STRATEGY #64
The Utah Biology Teacher

A few years ago after presenting a workshop in Salt Lake City, a teacher came up to me to share his story of how he dealt with a difficult class of ninth grade biology students. All of us in education can learn a lot from his experience.

Patrick (not his real name) was a first year teacher who taught six Biology classes a day. Five periods were going well, but his sixth period class was out of control. He dreaded facing that group every day. It bothered him so much that he contemplated quitting. One day, Lucinda, a veteran teacher at the school, heard Patrick talk about his sixth period class. Lucinda, recognizing Patrick's frustration responded, "Hey, sixth period is my planning period. Do you mind if I sit in the back of your room and work?" Lucinda and Patrick devised a couple simple rules concerning discipline issues. Every day for a few weeks, Lucinda sat in sixth period. Just her presence in the room had a positive impact on student behavior. She was also able to give Patrick advice. After a while, he gained the experience and confidence to handle the class on his own. Thanks to Lucinda, Patrick did not quit and eventually became a very successful teacher.

If you have a difficult class, seek advice from others. If you are one of those veteran teachers like Lucinda and you see a young teacher struggling, offer your support.

AHA! Quotes

1. "The one thing that I cannot accept is not trying."
   – **Michael Jordan**

2. "If I want something I've never had, I must do something I've never done."
   – **anonymous**

3. "Don't let obstacles stand in the way of your dreams."
   – **Muhammad Ali**

4. "It's your attitude, not your aptitude that determines your altitude."
   – **Zig Ziglar**

5. "Life's most persistent and urgent question is: What are you doing for others?"
   – **Martin Luther King Jr**.

6. "I've never seen an instance of one or two disputants convincing the other by arguing."
   – **Thomas Jefferson**

7. "Be kind. Everyone you meet is fighting a hard battle."
   – **John Watson**

8. "It is possible to have a brain and not a mind. A brain is inherited; a mind is developed."
   – **Reuven Feuerstein**

9. "I will never understand all the good a simple smile can accomplish."
   – **Mother Teresa**

10. "He who angers you, conquers you."
    – **anonymous**

11. "I destroy my enemy by making him my friend."
    – **Abraham Lincoln**

12. "No one thinks clearly when his fists are clinched."
    – **George Nathan**

13. "Good timing is making friends before you need them."
    – **anonymous**

14. "The time is always right to do what is right."
    – **Martin Luther King Jr**.

15. "It takes only one person to change your life – you."
    – **Ruth Casey**

16. "It's nice to be important, but it's more important to be nice."
    – **anonymous**

17. "You cannot truly listen to someone and do something else at the same time."
    – **M. Scott Peck**

18. "The ways of progress is neither swift or easy."
    – **Marie Currie**

19. "The friends you keep determines the trouble you meet."
    – **Chinese Proverb**

20. "Hold fast to your dreams, for if dreams die, life is a broken-winged bird that cannot fly."
    – **Langston Hughes**

STRATEGY #65
It's Unconditional

Quite often when teachers have difficult students, they try to find them jobs and responsibilities in hopes that it will help improve behaviors. Then what usually happens is this: Sixth grader Horace's behavior doesn't improve, so Mrs. Johnson doesn't let him go to tutor a first grader anymore. She may say, "Horace, how can I let you work with first graders when you can't behave?" I strongly believe that these challenging students can benefit from having special jobs. They should be given these jobs with no strings attached. Even if Horace's behavior doesn't change at first, he should be allowed to continue to work with the first graders, unconditionally. Once he realizes he can keep the job, then he will become even more responsible knowing he must show up daily. The more often he goes, the better his chances of feeling good about himself and eventually Mrs. Johnson will see improvement in his behavior. Remember, there are no quick fixes!

STRATEGY #66
You Could Have Done Worse

The next time your explosive, inflexible student loses control and pushes someone or throws a book down, start out by saying something positive. For example, "Jay, you could have done worse. At least you didn't hit her. Now we have to look at the consequences of your actions." This approach sends a message to the child that he does have "some" self-control and is making progress.

STRATEGY #67
What Do You Want?

Have you ever noticed the amount of time and energy adults put in trying to determine why a child is misbehaving? We know that children usually misbehave because they are trying to get their basic needs met or they just want something. Have you ever gotten so frustrated with a child that you yelled out, "What do you want?" You'll be surprised at the answers you get if you ask that question. Go ahead and try it next time. It may save you a lot of time and energy.

STRATEGY #68
From Class Clown to Class Comedian

At one time or another, all teachers have had to deal with a class clown. Although these students have a way of getting everyone's attention, we must not overlook the fact that having a good sense of humor is a gift. Many class clowns have ended up with successful careers that utilize their humor. I remember hearing President Clinton's humorist being interviewed and he noted, "The same things (telling jokes, acting silly) that got me sent to the principal's office when I was in school are the same things that got me sent to the White House today."

Instead of battling the class clown, use him to your benefit. Sit down with him and sign the Official Class Comedian Contract (see next page). Set terms and limits. For example, as a part of the contract, he may be allowed to tell two funny jokes a day, make a couple of silly comments, or take his comedy routine to the other classes once a week. Instead of squelching his talents and strengths, help him to use them to both of your advantages.

STRATEGY #69
Restitution: Making It Right!

According to *Webster's New Dictionary*, the word "restitution" means, "an act of restoring what was lost or taken away: a reimbursement, as for loss." It seems as though today we have so many young people taking away things from others. Yes, they take away or steal things, vandalize property, and even physically hurt others. Even worse, they take away people's dignity, respect, and self-esteem. Sometimes it appears that the victim suffers more than the person who commits the violation. I've seen students suspended for hitting an innocent victim. Sure, they received a strong consequence, but what about the victim who feels physical and emotional pain?

As teachers, we need to do all we can to help the victim. If Jayna breaks Lisa's pencil, what can she do to make it right? Does Jayna buy her a new pencil? When Larry pushes Hank down, how can Larry apologize or "make it right?" If you hear Luke making a racist remark to Jermaine, what can you do to encourage restitution? Too many youngsters get by with a slap on the fingers when they do wrong, but what about the victims?

Official Class Comedian
CONTRACT

Let it be known that on this date _____,

_____ *(name of student)* has been employed

as the Class Comedian in the class of _____

(teacher's name). This contract will be reviewed on a weekly basis. Either

party can cancel the contract at anytime.

As Class Comedian, I _____, agree to the following terms:

1.

2.

3.

4.

5.

6.

7.

8.

Signatures: _____

                _____

STRATEGY #70
Service First…School Second

Several school districts throughout the country have developed creative programs to address the needs of extremely disruptive students. One such program focuses on the belief that these challenging students can improve once they begin helping/serving others. One school district in southern Virginia takes a unique approach to getting students to help others. The school selected ten or twelve violent/aggressive students in the middle and high school. Before they get to school, they spend two hours every day at a nursing home, shelter for the homeless, a pre-school or a farm. The students begin to enjoy developing relationships with needy people and their self-esteems begin to rise as they see the impact they can have on others. After serving others for two-hours, they tend to come to school with better attitudes.

STRATEGY #71
The Bully Box

Bullies are sneaky. Seldom do they get caught and even more rarely do students tell on them. Just outside the counselor's office place a lock box called The Bully Box. Any student who is a victim of a bully or who witnesses a bully in action is encouraged to fill out a special form and drop it in the box (see next page). On the form the student is to briefly describe what happened, provide the names of victims and, of course, give the name of the bully. The date, time and location of the event is to be written down. The name of the student filling out the form is to be kept confidential. The school counselor is to empty the box on a regular basis and make note of the names of students who appear frequently on the forms. A plan of action needs to be made to confront the bullies.

STRATEGY #72
Freebies

As a school counselor, I sometimes have to meet with a student who isn't too excited about coming to my office. She may believe that she isn't the one with the problem; it's the teacher who is at fault. Getting to first base with a student like this can be a challenge. The following technique has proven successful with some of these students.

During the first visit I make an attempt to find out his/her interests. For instance, if Tyra tells me she likes horses, I search my inventory of freebies. Eventually I find a listing for a free

BULLYING INCIDENT REPORT

Name(s) of student(s) doing the bullying:_____
_____

Name(s) of victim(s):_____

What happened? When (time and date)? Where did it happen?

_____
_____
_____

Your name_____ *(your name will not be
used without permission)*

Drop this form in the Bully Box located_____

BULLYING INCIDENT REPORT

Name(s) of student(s) doing the bullying:_____
_____

Name(s) of victim(s):_____

What happened? When (time and date)? Where did it happen?

_____
_____
_____

Your name_____ *(your name will not be
used without permission)*

Drop this form in the Bully Box located_____

booklet on horses or maybe horse stickers. In her presence, I fill out the request for the freebies, put it in an envelope, attach a stamp, and walk with her to the office to put it in the out-going mail tray. I use her return address. This usually adds a bit of excitement as Tyra looks forward to getting her goodies in the mail and she realizes that I was the person responsible for ordering them. For the next few days I check with her to see if her package arrived. I get her to promise to show me her mail when she gets it. This simple activity helps me and Tyra develop a more personal relationship.

Keep a file of "freebies." Purchase books such as *Freebies for Kids*. Cut out articles for free things from the newspaper or magazines. All these resources prove beneficial in helping you and a difficult student connect.

STRATEGY #73
Strategic Planning

What is Strategic Planning? It involves situations where a student may misbehave, be defiant, be disrespectful, use bad language, or bully another student. You observe the poor behavior, but you realize that the child is so angry, so wound up that you may not be able to follow through with a consequence at that time, but you will give the student a consequence at a later time when the child is more under control. You strategically plan to implement the consequence at a later time.

Here are some examples:

1. On the way to the playground, Mary pushes Lance to the ground. You witness the event and respond by saying, "Mary, I saw that. Sit down for ten minutes before going back to play." She acts like she does not hear you and takes off for the swings. You say to yourself, "Do I go running after her? Will I have to restrain her? Maybe the principal isn't here today to help me." Instead you let her go, knowing that she still owes you ten minutes of time. The following day your class is lined up to go to the gym to watch a puppet show. On the way you stop at the principal's office and say to him, "Mr. Simpson, can Mary sit with you for the first ten minutes of the show?"

2. Eight grader Alvin was told to clean up the mess he left on the cafeteria floor. He looks at you and says, "I didn't make that mess!" He turns and walks out. Later that day you tell his wrestling coach that he will be late for practice because he still has a mess to clean up.

3. Twelve year old Martha is supposed to do dishes tonight. She keeps arguing with her mother about it. No matter how much mother threatens her, she refuses to do the dishes because, "I have too much homework!" Mother gets so frustrated that she says, "Okay, I don't want to listen to you fuss anymore. I'll do the dishes." It takes her 30 minutes to do Martha's dishes. Then on Friday night, Martha says to her mother, "Don't forget, I need to be at school by 7:00 for the football game." Mother replies, "Martha, you will be there at 7:30. Since I had to do your dishes, I'm running 30 minutes behind schedule this week."

STRATEGY #74
Changing Behaviors With Mnemonics

As educators, we are constantly trying to help young people improve their behavior. In most cases we are asking them to do something other than what they are used to doing. Johnnie has learned to hit those who hit him first. If someone calls Mollie a name she quickly returns the favor. If someone crowds ahead of Zeke, he then crowds ahead of other students. With the help of mnemonics we can help teach young people better ways to solve conflicts. The word "mnemonics" refers to, "assisting the memory" or "a technique of improving memory." By giving children quick and simple steps to follow, they are more apt to use them. For example, I taught my third graders to use their STP whenever they had a conflict on the playground. They knew that the S stood for: Stay cool, T: Think, and P: Practice the skills they were taught.

Here are some more examples of mnemonics:

- As parents we were encouraged to use the 4:1 principle. For every one negative thing we say to our children, we need to say at least four positive things.

- I trained many of my students to resolve conflicts by using the 6 C's of Conflict Resolution. They were able to remember these six steps because they all began with the letter C.

- Thomas Phelan's parenting model, *1,2,3 Magic* is a simple process that lets children know they have two chances to change their behavior before suffering a consequence.

STRATEGY #75
Downshifting

Have you ever been hesitant to say "no" to an impulsive, explosive child for fear of what might happen? In his book, *The Explosive Child*, Ross Greene suggests using a quick intervention known as downshifting. He notes, "In the same way that you wouldn't shift from fifth gear to reverse in one easy step in the car (unless you wanted to tear up a transmission), you shouldn't try the same thing with an inflexible-explosive child. What you should do instead is to try to shift the car (child) slowly from fifth gear to fourth, fourth to third, etc...." (p. 114). Here is an example:

Fourth grader Alex wants to play on his computer but has not finished his math yet.
Alex: "Mr. Lockhart, can I use the computer now?
Teacher: (instead of saying, "No, you don't have your math finished yet.")
"Alex, do me a favor and give this to the secretary. When you return, let me see how many math problems you have left. Don't worry, the computer is waiting for you."

STRATEGY #76
When Confrontation is Inevitable

Eventually you may have to confront the defiant student. When you do, be sure to consider the following:

Your Temperament: Take a close look at yourself first. Are you one who tends to get loud, coercive, or "wordy?" If you are too passionate, will it add fuel to the fire? On the other hand, if you are soft-spoken and not very assertive, will the student try to intimidate you?

The Child's Temperament: Are you knowledgeable of the child's temperament? Is Lonnie quick-tempered? Does he act very defensive? Do you have to say one or two positive things to him before you share your concern? If you get too loud, will he shut-down and refuse to talk?

Special Circumstances: Are there any crucial events happening in the child's life that you need to take in to consideration when a confrontation is inevitable? Will Lucinda be a bit touchy this week because she just found out that her parents are getting divorced? Could it be the reason that Luke seems much more quick to anger is because his father's drinking problem is getting worse?

Past Histories: Always consider past experiences with the child. The last time you and Cari had a meeting, what happened? How did she react? Did you follow through with your stated consequences? If you did not follow through the last time, then the student may not believe you this time. Also, did the student successfully complete his/her agreement?

Location: Where you and the student have a confrontation is very important. Is it safe to be in a room alone with Josh when you ask him about cheating on a test? Should you always be sitting behind your desk with the student standing or is it best to sit in chairs facing each other? Try not to confront the student in front of classmates. This could back-fire on you. You may want to consider different locations in the school. Could it be that sitting outside on a bench with Lindy gets better results than a gathering in the principal's office?

Also, consider the various roles you may have in the student's life. For instance, Mr, Henry is Mario's football coach and the lunch room monitor. On the football field, Mr. Henry can get quite tough with Mario. He may even yell at him. "That's it! Give me 20 push-ups!" Mario will accept it, but things are quite different in the cafeteria. If Mr. Henry has to reprimand Mario for bad behavior in the cafeteria when he is on duty, Mario may be less respectful, especially if his friends are watching.

Time of Day: Will it be best to confront Shanneka first thing in the morning or will it be best to wait until the end of the day?

Support: If you have to confront the student, will there be support? Is there a co-worker close by? Is your principal aware of the situation and is he/she going to help out if necessary? Have you developed a decent relationship with the student's parents and do you know they will back you up?

STRATEGY #77
Getting In Sync with the Out-Of-Sync Child

In 1998, Carol Kranowitz wrote the book, *The Out-Of-Sync Child* which described Sensory Integration Dysfunction (or SI Dysfunction) as the inability to process information received through the senses. Many students with SI Dysfunction can have challenging behavior problems such as being highly active, impulsive, easily distracted, and possible emotional problems. They also may have problems with muscle tone/motor coordination, poor eye-hand coordination, resistance to novel situations, and making transitions. Academic and social problems can occur. The book notes that between 12-30 percent of children today have SI problems significant enough to warrant intervention.

I strongly encourage you to read Kranowitz' book because it is very possible that you have students in your class with sensory processing problems. Once you become more aware of their processing problems, then you may be able to prevent some potential misbehaviors. Here are a few examples:

- For the child that doesn't like to be touched, let him be first or last in line. This lessens the opportunity of others bumping into him.

- Don't use strong smelling perfumes or after-shave lotion if you know you have a child sensitive to smell.

- Sometimes the "out of sync" child may get so wound up because of the sights and sounds in the room that he/she may crawl under the desk. Allow him/her this option.

- Special arrangements may be needed for taking tests. He/she may need an extremely quiet place.

- Try not to force children to eat or taste food items when they balk.

- Observe these children closely on the playground. They may do risky/dangerous things. Also, they may be victims of teasing because of their poor motor skills.

- Find out early if these children do or do not want to be hugged. Don't take it personally if Lenny says, "Don't touch me."

- Don't waste time arguing with Maurice when he says, "It's too hot," or "It's too cold in here."

- Be cognizant of the fact that some of these children cannot handle the noise or large areas of space in the gym or cafeteria.

- When they visit a new place, be patient. They will probably want to touch everything.

- If they smile or ignore you when you are fussing at them, don't get upset. They are often not good at picking up visual cues or facial expressions.

- Some of these children will tug, pull, and even chew on clothing that feels uncomfortable on their skin.

STRATEGY #78
The Great Switcheroo

When everything else fails...switch! Whatever you are trying isn't working, so try the opposite. A 180 degree turn may catch the student off-guard and could produce some positive changes. If you're usually quiet, get loud. If you always dress professionally, come to class in jeans and a t-shirt. If you always give Jenny a treat, ask her for a piece of candy. Take the class outside for a lesson. Play music in the back-ground. If you are always serious in nature, tell funny jokes. If you never touch the students, try surprising them with a hand-shake or a pat on the back. If you always take the class outside for play at one o'clock, take them out at nine. A sudden change of routine may be just what the doctor ordered!

STRATEGY #79
Nonviolent Crisis Intervention

Just as a policeman hopes and prays that he never has to use his gun, teachers desire never to have to restrain a student. Would you know how to properly restrain a child if he was hurting himself or others? Do you know specific strategies to use if you were attacked by a student? I strongly encourage educators to take the Nonviolence Crisis Intervention training through the <u>Crisis Prevention Institute, Inc.</u> (www.crisisprevention.com). You will learn numerous techniques such as: kick-block, hair-pull release, front choke release, bite release, children's control position, transport technique, and others.

STRATEGY #80
Helping Parents Weather the Adolescent Years

Even the best of parents struggle during their children's adolescent years. These mothers and fathers are constantly looking for help. Provide your parents with the handout "The Adolescent Years: Weathering the Storm." (see next page)

The Adolescent Years: Weathering the Storm

SUGGESTIONS FOR PARENTS...

1. Try not to be too critical of their actions, music, and clothing. Overly critical parents tend to raise overly angry children.

2. Psychiatrist Bruno Bettleheim noted, "During the period of adolescent turmoil, it is best when parents can accept their adolescent's odd, antagonistic or otherwise unpleasant behavior, without approving of it."

3. Update your parenting skills. What worked with Amy when she was six may not work when she is sixteen.

4. Talk to them as if they are adults. Include them in daily discussions about religion, politics, music and current events. Respect their opinions.

5. Stick to your values, but try not to take too active a role in asserting them. The more you try to pound your values into your children, the more they may rebel.

6. Let them win an occasional battle. If you let your son cut his hair the way he wishes, even though you do not approve of it, it may help you deal with him on more serious issues.

7. When times get stressful between you and your adolescent, send yourself to "time-out." Sometimes it is best to remove yourself before things get worse.

8. Set house rules, curfew, and consequences together – you and your adolescent. Always follow through with agreed consequences.

9. Expect challenges. There will be outbursts, tears, whining, and unpleasant remarks. Try to remain calm, state your view, don't argue, and stick to consequences.

10. Find time to talk with your adolescent. Use good timing. Sometimes the best time to talk could be while eating pizza and watching MTV at midnight.

11. Talk with other parents of adolescents. You'll find that they are dealing with many of the same issues you are.

12. Adolescents tend to be risk takers and may live dangerously at times, but they have a great need to return to a safe, nurturing home environment. Make sure you are providing such an environment.

13. Use the "Yes" Theory. Say "yes" as much as possible so they will be more likely to respect the "no."

14. Allow them to express anger, but encourage them to do it properly,

15. Be patient — this period will pass.

STRATEGY #81
The Freeze Technique for Students Who Refuse to Do Any Work

Dr. J. Allen Queen, author of *Responsible Classroom Management* suggests using the "Freeze Technique" for students who refuse to do any work. He encourages teachers to try this strategy for three to six weeks.

1. Students are informed that they are not being responsible.

2. Parents are sent a letter informing them that their children are not participating and after numerous attempts to get the child involved you have decided to spend time with students wishing to learn. As soon as each child decides to be a part of the class, you will assist them in any way to assure their academic success.

3. Place a chart with these students' names visible in the room.

4. Record in some manner every item of work not completed.

5. Refuse to give these students any attention — especially negative attention. Remember, you have been getting zero so why waste your energy and let others suffer. Zero is zero.

6. Now the good part. Once any of these students begin doing any work, positively encourage and unfreeze. Remove their names from the list once they get caught up.

STRATEGY #82
The Violent Student Meeting Checklist

Most of the time, teachers are likely to be in a classroom with others (i.e. students, assistants, other professionals) so, if a student becomes violent, there will be help available, as well as witnesses. But what about those who often have to meet with violent students in an office setting? For instance, counselors, principals, psychologists, social workers and other support personnel often find themselves alone with potentially dangerous individuals. The next time you have concerns going into a meeting, fill out the Violent Student Meeting Checklist (see next page), and just play it safe!

THE VIOLENT STUDENT MEETING CHECKLIST*

___ 1. Have a security plan in place. Alert the principals or public resource officers. Have an escape route.

___ 2. On your desk keep a bell, horn, or another loud sounding device to let others know you need help immediately.

___ 3. Keep squeeze balls, clay and other manipulatives on your desk.

___ 4. Take an occasional deep breath to help you stay calm.

___ 5. Do not let the student intimidate you.

___ 6. Keep snacks, candy, gum, or soda for you and the student to share.

___ 7. Always maintain a safe distance from the student.

___ 8. If the violent student attempts to leave the room or run out, let him go. Do not attempt to stop him.

___ 9. Do not make strong demands.

___10. Make sure your chair is close to the door.

___11. Do not point fingers or use threatening body language.

___12. Do not leave potential weapons (scissors, letter openers) on your desk.

___13. Learn which of your client's hands is dominant and keep to their weaker side.

___14. Have you considered taking self-defense classes?

___15. Do your best to end the meeting on a positive note.

*Adapted from, "Assessing Client Risk of Violence," by Lorna L. Hecker in *The Therapist's Notebook*, Hecker, Lorna and Deacon, Sharon. Haworth Press, New York, 1998.

STRATEGY #83
The Unteachables

Here is a unique, risky strategy that a middle school principal shared with me. He claims to have used it only four or five times and got positive results. This is definitely a strategy for when all else fails!

The disruptive seventh grader meets with the principal who says:

"Louis, your teachers inform me that you are not working and that you are always disrupting class. They are beginning to feel that you are unteachable. I find that hard to believe because at this school we have some of the best teachers in the state. They have successfully taught students who were visually and/or hearing impaired, kids with learning disabilities, slow readers, students with physical handicaps, and others with certain disorders. You seem to be a pretty smart young man at times but they can't seem to get to you. On my computer I have a list of all the unteachables at the school and as of today yours is the only name on the list. I'm confused about all of this. I think you are teachable. I want you to return to class and prove your teachers wrong. I'll check with them in a day or two and hopefully I'll be able to take your name off my list."

STRATEGY #84
Quick, Hand Me That Camera!

I heard of a middle school principal that was very concerned about the number of fights at his school. He was also bothered by the numbers of students who gathered in circles to watch. The fighters and the other students often scattered before being caught. Things improved greatly when he supplied all teachers and staff with disposable cameras. They were told to grab the cameras and rush to the halls when they heard a fight. Their snapshots proved valuable when confronting the fighters and their audiences!

STRATEGY #85
It Doesn't Hurt to Ask

Let's say that you've tried every trick in the book in an attempt to get Rhonda to behave better in class. Nothing has worked and you prefer not to keep sending her to the office. Try this.

Go to your principal and ask, "Can I have permission to call Rhonda's parents whenever I feel she needs to be sent home? Also, am I allowed to try an occasional Tolerance Day?" Note here: Tolerance Day is a term used in *Reality Therapy* by Dr. William Glasser in which a student's parents are told to not allow their child to go to school for a day. The child is not really suspended; he/she is to stay home for a day to think about his/her behavior and to hopefully return with a better attitude. Many principals will agree to this idea as long as you keep them informed/updated.

STRATEGIES #86-91
Attack-Tics*

Conflict is not a contest. Winning and losing are goals for games, not conflicts. If your goal is to win the conflict or confrontation, you may be fighting a losing battle. For instance, if you say to a student, "Mary, keep your mouth closed. I don't want to hear another word. I know you were the one who took the pen off my desk!" Mary follows your order, she keeps quiet but, did you really win or will Mary seek revenge or lose respect for you if, in fact, she didn't take your pen?

At times educators are subjected to many conflicts, confrontations, verbal abuse and, unfortunately, physical attacks. Following are six options or ATTACK-TICS, to use when being attacked, physically or verbally.

*The term Attack-Tics is adapted from, *Aikido in Everyday Life: Giving in to Get Your Way*, by Terry Dodson and Victor Miller, North Atlantic Books, Berkeley, CA 1978.

STRATEGY #86
Confluence

First, you must join with the attacker. Get alongside him or her. Agree with their right to feel whatever it is they are feeling. You are not necessarily agreeing with them about everything, but it certainly won't cost you anything to empathize. Become confluent. After all, the student may be in the wrong, but you can't argue with the obvious fact that he/she is upset. Confluence can be used to deal with any attack at any time and any place.

Examples:
Student: "You are the most boring teacher I've ever had!"
Teacher: "Well I know that sometimes being a student is the pits."

Student: "You make me so mad sometimes that I feel like hitting something!"
Teacher: "I don't blame you for getting frustrated. Algebra is hard and I tend to really push my students to do their best."

STRATEGY #87
Deception

Deception is to be used when you want to surprise your opponent, break his/her line of intention. There are two kinds of Deception.

Diversion: **Putting Up a Smokescreen...**
This simply means getting the attacker off his/her original mission by surprising him/her and offering something else to look at. An example would be a second grade teacher saying to a hostile student, "Look at the size of that bird! I've never seen one that big before." That small bit of deception or distraction may defuse the angry child.

Deflection: **The White Lie...**
Most would agree that honesty is the best policy but, who could blame a potential rape victim for telling the attacker, "I've got AIDS."? A classroom example would be this. Mr. Hansen, Biology teacher, looking at his watch as a verbally abusive student gets loud says, "Oh, it's ten o'clock. Principal Jones is supposed to be here for a visit. Does anyone see him coming?"

STRATEGY #88
Doing Nothing

Doing Nothing is appropriate when you need time. It is also an appropriate response when you want to find out what's really behind the attack. Doing Nothing is one of the best responses when the attack makes no sense, when it is totally absurd. Authors Dodson and Miller remind us, "In order to use Do Nothing as an effective response to conflict, the first step is to get over any lingering doubts you may have about bravery or lack of it. Remember, you choose to Do Nothing. You don't Do Nothing because you're afraid to do something, and you don't lose face if you know inside that the choice to Do Nothing was your own." (p.69)

STRATEGY #89
Parley

Parley is a reasoned exchange of possible solutions, the discussion of possible outcomes. Parley is most effective when you are in a no-win situation. Here is an example.
Student: "You're not fair! Mrs. Harrington never gives us homework on weekends!"
Teacher: "Well, tell me what's wrong with having a bit of homework on the weekends?"

When you Parley, you buy time. It opens an exchange of thoughts and ideas that help defuse the student. Police officers are taught that the longer a felon or potential suicide is kept talking, the greater the chance for mutual survival.

STRATEGY #90
Withdrawal

To withdraw means to calmly and slowly walk away from the attacker. Withdrawal is appropriate when all else fails and an escape route is open to you. Withdraw when the time and place are wrong.

STRATEGY #91
Fighting Back

Fighting Back should be your last alterative after you have decided that there is no Withdrawing, no chance of Parley, for Deception, or for Confluence, and you must do something. Fighting Back is your last resort. Aikido experts and authors Dodson and Miller note, "And we're quite serious about that. You have to learn to resist the first impulse to lash out wildly at your attacker. There are many cases where people have fought a mugger and lost their lives. Had they chosen another response, they might have lived." (p. 38). Fight Back when it is a question of life or death (yours or someone else's) and you have no other options.

STRATEGY #92
Sorry, Contract Denied!

Warning:
Some teachers may feel uncomfortable with this strategy, but it has proven very effective.

Often teachers send disruptive students to a counselor or principal to draw-up contracts or plans to improve behavior. The student then returns to the class with a plan that the teacher almost always accepts or approves. Some teachers are uncomfortable with this process because they feel that it may give the student the message that, "I can't handle you so I need to send you to the principal. Maybe he can get you to behave better in class." These teachers may feel a loss of power. Here is a strategy for writing contracts that helps the teacher maintain his/her power.

Fifth grade teacher, Mrs. Haas, has tried everything she could to help Chris improve/change his behavior, but nothing seemed to work and she was getting very frustrated. She and I met and agreed on a strategy. I told her to send him to me to develop a contract. She was instructed not to accept the plan. In fact, I told her to keep sending him back to write new ones. No matter what the contract noted, she was to turn them down. Chris returned to the class with a new plan and she said, "No, I don't like this plan. It's not good enough. I need a tougher one before I let you back in class." Chris soon became frustrated. I remember him saying to me after his fifth trip, "Even if the superintendent wrote a plan today, she wouldn't sign it!" Finally, I called her and told her to accept the next plan. This "trick" sent a powerful message to Chris. He realized that it was the teacher, not someone from the office, that had the final say in allowing him to return to her class.

STRATEGY #93
Personalized Prescriptions

Homework issues can become a problem for many disruptive students. They have trouble completing the work, they may not have anyone at home to help them, or they refuse to do it. Should your academically gifted Juan be given the same homework assignments as your ODD, LD student Jimmy? You may have to make adjustments with some of your more difficult students. For instance, Lindy is very capable of writing a two-page report on the Hopi Indians but Skip struggles in writing. Skip is good with his hands. Why not let him build a small Hopi teepee or totem pole? Chuck is probably unable to complete tonight's long division problems. Instead of making him do the same assignment as the rest of the class, give him a personalized homework prescription/assignment. Tell him to watch the Lakers' game and determine Shaquille O'Neal's foul-shooting percentage.

Personalized prescriptions are individualized assignments, duties, and responsibilities to help those students who may not be capable of doing what most other students are. Get creative.

Know the strengths of your students and have them utilize those strengths to complete goals and objectives. I'll never forget the day I had third-grader Justin research the values of three of my most valued baseball cards. He completed the assignment successfully by finding the necessary information. I then gave him math assignments that involved batting averages, pitcher's earned run averages, and other baseball statistics. He would always get excited when I wrote him another personalized prescription. He didn't realize, at first, that he was mastering math in a completely different way than his peers.

STRATEGY #94
1-3-1 Plans

Most students are rather receptive to writing/signing behavior plans and contracts. They look forward to receiving rewards and praise for improving their conduct. However, with Oppositional Defiant Disorder students, you need to get more creative. For example, Stephen thinks writing a contract with a teacher is "stupid" and probably won't live up to his terms of the agreement because he doesn't want to have his behavior controlled by a person in a position of authority. ODD students like to challenge and confront teachers and other adults. Individualized one-on-one plans seldom work with ODD students.

With difficult students, try using what I call 1-3-1 Plans. This is how it works. I'll use a fifth grader named Alvin for an example.

1. I meet with Alvin and discover that he loves playing basketball but he tells me that he has no kids in his neighborhood to play ball with him on weekends and after school.

2. I ask him to give me the names of three other students at school that he would like to play basketball with if I can arrange a time.

3. I get him to agree on improving one aspect of his behavior for five days. He agrees not to "talk back."

4. I invite the three students he named to meet with Alvin and me. They also sign the contract and they realize that if Alvin successfully completes his agreement they get to play some two-on-two basketball. I supervise and schedule their game.

I've had much success with these plans because the ODD child sees that he is doing better, not to impress me (the adult), but for his friends. (see next page)

1-3-1 PLAN

Date_____

People involved in plan:

    1) Student _____

    2) Friends_____

    3) Teacher/Counselor/Principal_____

Terms of contract: _____

_____

_____

The signing of our names signifies that we all agree to the terms of this contract.

_____   _____

_____   _____

_____   _____

1-3-1 PLAN

Date_____

People involved in plan:

    1) Student _____

    2) Friends_____

    3) Teacher/Counselor/Principal_____

Terms of contract: _____

_____

_____

The signing of our names signifies that we all agree to the terms of this contract.

_____   _____

_____   _____

_____   _____

STRATEGY #95
Make Saving Students a Community Effort

Most schools try to resolve discipline problems on their own while a few get creative and involve other agencies in the communities. One such school district joined forces with their county's parks and recreation department and the local police department. Together, they shared finances, personnel, and facilities.

This is how the program works. The school, with parental permission, selects students in grades 5-8 who display violent, aggressive, and defiant behaviors. These students arrive at their base school each morning and then bussed to a camp located in the country. The camp and building facilities are donated by the parks and recreation department. The camp is run by teachers (from the public schools) and police officers. Strict rules and dress codes are enforced. At the camp they do much physical labor as well as a fair amount of schoolwork. During a normal day, a student might mop floors, paint a wall, work in the yard, and then do some reading. At the end of each day they are bussed back to their base schools. The students must earn their way out of the program.

A similar program is being used in Rock Hill, South Carolina. Their program is called "Rebound" and claims to have an 85% success rate.

STRATEGY #96
Chauffeur Please!

Instead of suspending Jameka for five days, sentence her to five days of "chauffeuring." For five days she will not be allowed to be without extremely close adult supervision.

- Her parent(s) must drive her to school and pick her up at the end of the day.

- Her parent(s) are to walk her to class.

- If she is involved in an after-school activity, a parent must be present.

- A teacher, assistant, volunteer, or other staff members take turns sitting next to her in class. They will actually "shadow" her.

- She must sit with an adult at lunch.

- She will be escorted in the halls.

- She will not be allowed to go to the bathroom with her class. She will be escorted to the bathroom when other students aren't using it.

This may seem extreme, but it's still better than suspension. Most parents would prefer this over having to make plans for supervising the suspended child at home.

STRATEGY #97
A Half-Day Will Do

Many aggressive, disruptive, and oppositional young people cannot handle a whole day of school. They might make it through math and reading classes, but when they get involved in less structured activities such as playtime and lunch, their behavior problems escalate. With some of these more extreme cases, schools have made arrangements to allow these students to leave school in the middle of the day. While at school in the morning, they concentrate on their core subjects. Yes, these few students will miss out on lunch with their peers and not attend elective/special classes but at least they are still going to school every day.

STRATEGY #98
The Teacher as Coordinator

At one time or another, every teacher gets a classroom full of students who have unusual personalities and temperaments. No matter what strategies the teacher implements, the students continue to clash. The teacher often says something like, "Individually, every kid is neat but when they are all in the room together, look out! They just can't get along and it isn't easy to teach."

Kindergarten teacher, Mrs. Hansen had one of those "personality-clashing" classes one year. By the end of September she had tried everything. The twenty-six children struggled to get along. After days of brainstorming she finally came up with a plan. She decided that for a while she would switch from being a teacher to being a coordinator. She made arrangements to have at least three or four volunteers in her room everyday. One person would take a group to the library, another went to the reading lab, while another adult would read stories to a small group. By breaking up the class into smaller groups and by getting many of the students separated things began to improve. Mrs. Hansen also scheduled guest speakers, storytellers, and had the school counselor visit on a regular basis to work on social skills. She invited the principal, school board members, and central office folks to work in her room. Mrs. Hansen's creativity and coordinator skills helped her survive a tough group.

STRATEGY #99
Boot Camps or Monasteries?

Let's say that we've tried everything possible to keep Dustin in school but nothing seems to have helped. It's time to look at another setting. Does he need a tough, prison-like setting such as a boot camp or would he benefit from a monastic model program? Let's compare the two. Boot camps are operated like a penitentiary for hard-core criminals. Youngsters are yelled at, humiliated, forced to run and do exercises, and punished severely for small violations. Their meals are served to them three times a day, they are seldom allowed to socialize, and if they have free time they are allowed to listen to music with violent lyrics or watch negative television shows or videos. They rarely get time for mediation or creativity. In a monastic-like setting there is no yelling, screaming, humiliation and/or put-downs by the leaders. Participants are not exposed to certain types of music and no television viewing is allowed. They must work in the garden and take care of animals. If they wish to eat, they must help prepare the food. They are allowed time for mediation and spiritual growth. The setting strives to be calm and peaceful. Time is allowed for positive interaction with others. They are allowed to pursue arts, crafts, or hobbies.

Which program do you feel will yield the best long-term results? In his book, *Lost Boys*, James Garbarino says this about boot camp, "These programs usually mimic military basic training: a lot of shouting, a lot of threats, powerful leaders who dominate new recruits through the force of their personality and sometimes with violence....I reject it as a model, because I think it is most unsuited for violent boys, given where they come from psychologically and who they are developmentally and spiritually....Psychiatrist Bruce Perry agrees that the last thing a boy with a traumatic psychological history needs is someone getting in his face and screaming at him." (p. 232)

STRATEGY #100
Parents, Don't Ever Forget…

During the past few years I have asked 1,801 third, fourth, and fifth graders the following question:

"Which of these statements would you prefer to hear most often from your parents?"

A) I love you.   B) I'm proud of you.

The results are startling. Almost 80% of the children selected A, I love you!

Parents must constantly tell their children that they are loved, unconditionally. Children need to know that they come first; their school performance is secondary. If Dawn thinks that her parents care more about her grades than they do about her as a person, look out. If Dawn feels that mom and dad are so concerned about her grades, she may rebel and allow her grades to suffer. The late psychiatrist, Bruno Bettleheim, had this to say in his book, *The Good Enough Parent*, "Our child may come to feel that we are only interested in his academic standing, and not him as a person. This may induce him to hate his studies, which he believes are more important to us than he is. It is but one of many situations in which a parent is sure that all he cares about is his child, while the child is sure his parents care only about his achievement, not for him… it is the great disappointment he experiences when he believes that we are more concerned with his performance than we are with him as a person. In consequence, he may come to resent school and all it stands for, to hate schoolwork to the degree he is actually unable to do it." (p. 62)

Special Featured Strategy:

THE BACK-UP UNIT

STRATEGY #101

The "Back-Up" Unit
An Unconventional, No-Nonsense Approach For Dealing With Disruptive Students

In today's society we often refer to "back-up" systems. Many of us have learned the hard way to always have a back-up on our computer for important documents. Here in North Carolina, many home owners have a generator for a back-up when they lose their power because of hurricanes. In the news we hear of reports that the police had to call in a back-up unit in a dangerous situation. Also, doctors and nurses call for back-ups in life and death matters. I believe that teachers, today more than ever, need a back-up system to help them deal with difficult students. Often, they need "extra" help and support as their classrooms contain a growing number of students who are struggling with various disorders such as attention deficit/hyperactivity disorder, Asperger's disorder, sensory integration dysfunction, depression, obsessive compulsive disorder, oppositional-defiant disorder, learning disabilities and others. So many of our children are "sensory addicted" and become easily bored or lazy. Often these challenging students disrupt class and teachers need a place to send them for various periods of time to help them regain control. The Back-Up Unit provides teachers with such a place.

Most teachers would agree that numerous back-up systems used is schools today are not very effective. Suspending students seldom changes behavior. Many schools that have time-out rooms do not use them properly as they become a dumping ground for silly behaviors and most of the time the students would rather be in the time-out room than in class. My travels throughout the country have taught me that a good number of teachers are not that supportive of in-school suspension programs. The lack of parental support also adds frustration as teachers try to work on student behaviors.

For many teachers, the only option is to look to the school office and/or principal for support with working with disruptive students. However, even this strategy is seldom effective. Discipline expert Fred Jones, in his book, *Positive Classroom Discipline* noted, "The reason a teacher is better off not relying on the office is because the office is inherently unreliable." (p. 292) By answering the following questions you will better understand what Jones is trying to say.

- Have you ever sent a disruptive student to the office and wondered what happened to him?
- Have you ever sent a rude, disrespectful student to the office and later saw her running an errand for the secretary?
- Were there times you needed to send a student to the office but realized that the principal was unavailable?
- Have you ever noticed that some students think it's "cool" to be sitting in the office and they grin to their peers as they go by?
- Do you feel sorry for the secretary who has to keep an eye on the challenging students until the principal gets time to see them?

The Back-Up Unit to be described is organized, operated and staffed by various school personnel. The room is always open and seldom will the principal be involved. The Back-Up Unit is a no-nonsense approach for working with students who are keeping the teacher from teaching and students from learning. This effective program should take care of 95% of the discipline problems in the school. For serious misbehaviors (i.e. fighting, weapons, drugs, open defiance, etc.) the students must be sent to the office.

So, What Exactly is the Back-up Unit and What Makes it so Unconventional?

- As noted, the Back-Up Unit is a small room where teachers can send disruptive students. It provides a strong message to the student, "I can't teach with you behaving that way. Go to the Back-Up Unit and I'll deal with you later!"

- The room is not overly comfortable. The door is always closed, no windows, dull coloring, and quiet. No one can see in or out of the room. The room must be as "calming" as possible. Many classrooms are full of bright colors, posters, cute animals, and toys, and things hanging from the ceiling. In our sensory addicted society, this provides too much stimulation for some children. The Back-up Unit must be as non-stimulating as possible!

- Students are to receive no attention at all! Why give these students any attention at this time? They were sent there because they were interfering with the rights of others to learn.

- In this room, the students sit in study carrels where they can't see others. I recommend one carrel per one-hundred students at the school. My experience finds that the fewer carrels you have, the better. If teachers know you have room for twenty, the more visitors you will get. Just the opposite is true; if teachers know space is limited, they are more selective in sending students.

- Students are not allowed to eat, talk or do schoolwork. They are still responsible for the work they miss. They are to sit quietly and hopefully, think. There is a powerful Native American quote that says, "Silence is the cornerstone of character."

- Students are not to receive counseling at this time. Many students will misbehave on purpose just to get sent to some time-out rooms because they'll receive special attention. They know that someone will talk with them and even help them with their math. Once again, Back-Up Unit visitors are not to receive any attention! They are reminded that, at other times, there are people who will help them (i.e. counselors, social workers, etc.). Students are encouraged to and told how they can contact these helpers but, in the Back-Up Unit they are on their own.
- The Back-Up Unit is always staffed and supervised.

- Most time-out rooms and in-school suspension rooms are headed up by one person. In these types of rooms, quite often the supervisor gets "burn-out" or develops special relationships with the disruptive students to the point that students may, again, misbehave on purpose just to see the supervisor/counselor. For example, Joe would prefer to be with Mr. Hampson in ISS than be in Miss Williams' math class. The Back-Up Unit is staffed by up to twenty different people a week. Because there is a different person staffing the room every 30-45 minutes, the students do not know who will be in the room. I have also found that most staff members do not mind being called on to supervise the room for these short time frames. They know they will have to cope with extremely difficult students but, for only few minutes a week, instead of, like some ISS folks, six hours a day, five days a week!

- There is almost no paperwork involved and teachers do not have to worry about sending work with the student.

- This system is very unconventional because it costs no extra money to operate.

- The Back-Up Unit is adaptable to almost any classroom management system/program that teachers are using.

- This program gives teachers more control/power. They are able to get the point across to the disruptive student that they (the teachers) can resolve these problems without always involving the principal.

- The Back-Up Unit has its own back-up. Students who refuse to go to this room or choose to misbehave while in there are sent to the office. Principals tend to be very firm with these individuals. Most students would rather go to the unit for a short period of time than have to deal with the principal.

The Importance of the Name

The term, Back-Up Unit, is appropriate for several reasons. First, of all, it has a serious tone to it. A student is sent there because his/her behavior caused the teacher to get backed-up in his/her lessons. The term also sends a message to the student that there is a place to send him/her for a short period of time. The term "time-out" is used so often now in schools and in homes that the students don't take it seriously. This is why I don't think a room in a school should be called a time-out room. Time-out within a class is fine, but an out of class room needs to have a different label. Finally, by selecting the term "Back-Up Unit," we've avoided the "cutesy" terms that some schools use. I've heard of the Tiger Room, Chill-out Room, Zoo, Jungle, Panda Room, and the Hug and Handshake Room. Students need to know that disrupting the class is serious and that they are not going to a warm and fuzzy room to cool down and get special attention!

Staffing

The best way for me to describe the staffing of the unit is to explain how it is accomplished at Cameron Park Elementary School in Hillsborough, North Carolina. When I first came to the school as a counselor in 1993, teachers were very concerned about discipline. They realized there was no money in the budget to pay for a person to operate a time-out room, but they all agreed that something had to be done. I put on my creative thinking cap and came up with an idea. I knew the school had nearly seventy employees which included teachers, assistants, and support personnel. I proposed this question at a faculty meeting, "If we all agree we need a room to send disruptive students, are we all willing to do our share to staff it?" I received an overwhelming, "Yes!" Soon a schedule was devised. I agreed to watch the room a half-hour a day. All teachers in grades K-3 agreed to allow their assistants to do one shift a week. Several support staff helped out and on occasion a parent volunteer or two chipped in. Every year, for ten years now, we have been able to keep the Back-Up Unit going without any additional money or personnel. One important note here: Even though teachers, assistants and others spend one shift a week in the room, they are not wasting time. While they are in there they can still do lesson plans, grade papers, and do other school-related work.

A similar type of room used in some schools is called the ICU (Intensive Care Unit). I am aware of some high-schools that staff the room in a very unique way. All teachers have one planning period a day or ten planning periods in a two week span. At one high school, each teacher agrees to spend one planning period every two weeks in the ICU. Again, while in there they keep busy with necessary lesson plans, grading, etc. I am also aware of several middle schools who have developed their own special room for disruptive students. They also implemented creative strategies for staffing the room.

The Process

Following are all the necessary steps to use when implementing an effective Back-Up Unit.

1. As a staff, all teachers must agree on what constitutes as a disruption. This is crucial for matters of consistency. Most educators would agree that the following behaviors are disruptions: throwing things, constantly out of seat, bothering others, making silly noises, continually blurting out responses, and pushing others. On the other hand, these behaviors technically are not to be considered as disruptions because they do not keep the teacher from teaching and other students from learning: sleeping in class, not working, or forgetting to bring a pencil to class. Once again, serious behaviors, such as fighting, must be referred to the office.

2. Teachers should try every strategy they can within their room before using the Back-Up Unit.

3. When a teacher sends a student to the unit, he/she must fill out a "Back-Up Unit Form." A sample form is included in this section of the book. On the form the teacher writes the student's name, time of day, and a time for when the student can return to class. The teacher does not have to write a description of the child's disruption on this form unless he/she wants a letter sent to parents. Students in kindergarten and first grade usually sit in the unit for ten minutes. Students in upper grades sit for an average of 15-30 minutes. With special permission from the principal or a parent, I've had students sit for up to two hours. The supervisor has the authority to keep a student for a longer period of time if he/she feels the student has not calmed down enough.

4. Within a few weeks of opening all students will know the location of the Back-Up Unit. 98% of the students sent to the unit will go on their own, carrying the form. Often teachers will call the unit to let them know a student is on the way. Yes, there will be a student or two who refuse to leave the room. Options for this dilemma include calling the principal or carrying the child to the unit. Each school should have trained employees who are certified in crisis prevention who know how to transport students. I recommend interested individuals to attend training through the Crisis Prevention Institute, Inc. (www.crisisprevention.com)

5. When students arrive at the unit, they hand the form to the supervisor and sit in a carrel. There should be no talking by anyone! The supervisor has a form to record student names, when they arrived, and when they returned to class. At the end of the day a copy of this form is given to the principal. The school counselor should check the daily logs to note names of frequent visitors.

6. A phone must be in the unit for communication purposes.

7. If a child is very out of control and needs restraining, the supervisor should call for help.

8. People staffing the room must be patient, understanding, and flexible with some students. For example, an extremely hyper-active kindergartener may not be able to sit quietly for ten minutes. Use your best judgment.

9. If a child falls asleep in the room, that's all right but, he must be awaken and told to leave the room when his time is up. I have noticed that many students are behavior problems because they don't get enough sleep.

10. If a student returns from the unit and his/her behavior hasn't changed, he/she should be sent back for a longer period of time.

11. Explain to the students that if they are sent to the unit and no one is on duty, they should report to the office.

12. With teacher's permission, students may request to go to the unit on their own if they need a place to cool down.

13. At any time a teacher may request a meeting with a counselor or principal to write a plan to address a student's behavior.

Final Thoughts

After almost ten years of having a Back-Up Unit at my school I've learned the following.

1. The unit does not work for every child. Every year I have one or two students who will not go to the unit for some reason. Alternate plans had to be made.

2. Every year I have four or five students who are regular visitors. Their behavior may not change, but at least they are somewhere else instead of back in their regular classrooms disrupting things.

3. Some teachers may go a whole year and never use the room. Other years those same teachers may use the room often because they may have more challenging students.

4. Because we've had the program at Cameron Park for ten years, it has become a permanent fixture. Parents know about it, most students have no desire to visit, and teachers always feel a bit more confident knowing there's a place to send Beverly when she gets out of control.

5. Busy secretaries and principals are less stressed out and can do their valuable duties without always seeing a bunch of students sitting on the bench waiting to see the "boss."

6. Here is what I like best about the Back-Up Unit. Over the years I've seen students get upset and do something inappropriate like throw a book on the floor, push someone down, backtalk, knock over a desk, or use profanity. Often these students were suspended. My observations find that when these kids "lose it," they tend to settle down in a few minutes and are ready to return to their schoolwork. I hate seeing students sent home for two days when they lost control for two minutes. With the Back-Up Unit they can sit, think about their behaviors, calm down, and return to class. Here again, I'm talking about those students who lack self-control, over react, and are impulsive. They don't always need to be sent home. I can be somewhat more patient and tolerant of those students of whom we have many. More serious consequences are needed for those students who know what they are doing and have the ability to control their actions.

The Cameron Park Story

In the summer of 1993 I attended an exciting and informative workshop at the University of North Carolina at Charlotte. The presenter, Dr. J. Allen Queen, discussed his Responsible Classroom Management program for teachers. In his presentation he talked about a time-out room called the ICU (Intensive Care Unit). I returned to Cameron Park Elementary School with several good ideas and eventually created our own special room. I took Queen's basic concept for his ICU but changed two things. Unlike the ICU, I would have only one person staffing the room at a time, unlike his recommendation of two. Also, in Queen's ICU a student is allowed to talk with an adult and devise a plan. In our new Back-Up Unit there would be no counseling and/or writing plans. The Back-Up Unit started with the 1993-1994 school year and is still in operation at the time of this writing (the 2002-03 school year).

Take time to study the following statistics on Cameron Park's Back-Up Unit's usage. Note that during the first year we had nearly thirty students a day visiting the room. As a staff we made a few changes and adjustments and continued the program. For the next eight years there was a continual decrease in the number of disruptive students visiting the unit.

School Year	Visitors to the Unit	Avg. # of Visitors Per Day
1993-1994	5204	28.8
1994-1995	1270	7.9
1995-1996	1328	8.2
1996-1997	1023	7.1
1997-1998	1028	7.1
1998-1999	1202	7.5
1999-2000	788	5.4
2000-2001	849	5.7
2001-2002	463	4.1

Breakdown By Grade Level For Past Nine Years

Grade	Total % of Visitors
K	8.8%
1	14.0%
2	23.8%
3	20.4%
4	13.1%
5	19.9%

More Interesting Facts:
- Busiest day of the week: Thursday
- Slowest day of the week: Monday
- Busiest month of the year: March or April
- Slowest month of the Year: September
- Busiest time of the day: 80% of visitors go between 12:30 and 1:45
- Most visitors by grade level: for 7 of the last 9 years, second graders were the most frequent visitors

Reasons for the Success of Cameron Park's Back-Up Unit

1. There was a total commitment of the faculty and staff to share in the operation of the unit.

2. The school has had three different principals during the past ten years. All of them have been supportive and have allowed the program to continue.

3. The school has persevered. Even after the first tough year, it stuck with the program. This is rare in today's schools. It seems that every year there are new programs. If one thing doesn't work one year, throw it out and try something new. Even Dr. William Glasser has noted that if you wish to change your school from an average school to a Quality School, it will take 3-5 years. How often do schools ever stay with a program that long?

4. Parents have been very supportive of the program. They agree that disruptive students need to be in school as much as possible. The Back-Up Unit keeps most of these students in school and cuts down on suspensions.

5. Teachers, parents, administration and others in the community have seen the positive results of the program. Not only are disruptions and suspensions down, but the school has received several special recognitions from the state of North Carolina for improvement on test scores. For the last four years, Cameron Park has been named as a School of Distinction.

BACK-UP UNIT FORM

Please admit _____

Person sending student _____

Date _____ Time of day _____

Please check one box below:

☐ Please let the student sit in the Back-Up Unit for a few minutes.
Send student back to class at _____ (time)
Or I will come for student at _____ (time)

☐ This student was disrupting class. Action needs to be taken. Please
send a letter home to parents. Send student back to class at _____
or I will come for student at _____.

Brief description of disruption: _____

_____

_____

_____

Comments/Suggestions: _____

_____

_____

_____

BACK-UP UNIT DAILY LOG

Student Name	Grade	Time Arrived	Time Left	Person Sending Student

Date _____

SAMPLE LETTER TO PARENTS

Cameron Park Elementary School
240 St. Mary's Road
Hillsborough, NC 27278

Dear Parent/Guardian:

    The purpose of this letter is to inform you that your child, _____, was sent to the Back-Up Unit (the school's time-out room) on _____ (date) for disrupting class. He/she was sent from the classroom because _____

_____

_____

    He/she lost several minutes of valuable instruction time. We appreciate your cooperation and please continue to let your child know the importance of behaving well. At Cameron Park we stress the importance of not allowing students to keep the teachers from teaching and other students from learning.

    If you have any questions or concerns please contact _____ at the school at _____ (phone #).

Sincerely,

Cameron Park
Discipline Committee

APPENDIX

An Alaskan Adventure

Listening is a very important skill. Many people are able to master this skill, while others never learn. Parents and teachers are constantly reminding children to listen and pay attention. I always remind my students, "Good things happen to good listeners and bad things happen to bad listeners." Chuck was not a good listener and something very bad happened to him. Let me tell you his story.

Chuck was a 35-year-old amateur photographer who had always dreamed of going to Alaska to take pictures. After several years, he was able to save enough money to quit his regular job and head to Alaska for a few weeks. Chuck never really took the time to learn much about Alaska before the trip. He was unaware of the extreme weather conditions and the great vastness of this state. He thought he was prepared for his trip. As we later find out, he was not prepared.

A few days before leaving, he had to get his hunting and fishing license, and take a safety/ rescue course. At the session, he never really listened or paid attention. He thought he knew everything he would need to know. He should have listened closely to rescue information, but he did not.

A bush plane dropped Chuck and his supplies off in the middle of one of the most remote areas of the state. He forgot to tell the pilot when to return to pick him up. For the next few weeks, he enjoyed the great outdoors and took many beautiful pictures. Soon his supplies began to run low. He was running out of food and the weather was turning cold.

Chuck still assumed that someone would eventually find him. Surely another hunter or bush plane would pass his way. He was getting ill and very weak and winter was close at hand. He began to really worry now. "Will I ever be rescued, and will I ever see my family again?" He could not hold out much longer.

As he was nearing death one day, he heard a plane. He dragged himself into an opening. The plane flew low and the pilot waved to him. Chuck was so excited that he raised his right hand in the air and pumped it up and down a few times just as a football fan would do after his team scored a touchdown. "I'm going to be rescued!" He went back to his shelter and started packing. Soon he would be back home with his family. He waited for the plane to return.

Several hours went by, then several days went by, and the plane did not return. Chuck knew the plane saw him. "The pilot actually waived to me." Something is wrong he thought. He huddled in the corner of his small shelter trying to keep from freezing. He was now completely out of food.

A couple more days went by without any sight or sound of the plane. With the last bit of energy he had, he took out his wallet to look at his family pictures one last time. He also took out his hunting license. As he read the back of his license, he discovered the reason for the plane not returning to help. On the license were drawings of emergency hand signals for communicating with aircraft from the ground. He discovered too late that raising a single arm is the universally recognized signal for, "All OK; assistance not necessary." The signal for, "SOS, send immediate help," is two upraised arms. Chuck used the wrong hand signal. He should have listened and paid attention when getting his license.

A few days later he died. We know the story of Chuck because he kept a diary which was recovered from his frozen shelter. If he had listened, he would have survived, but as a result – his actions were fatal.

From Monday Morning Messages by Tom Carr (www.youthlight.com)

A Tale of Determination

Ed and Donna were very exited. They were waiting the birth of their first child. Not only was Donna going to deliver any day, so was the neighbor's dog. On April 17th, Donna went to the hospital to give birth to a new baby boy, Danny. On the same day, Ginger, the neighbor's dog, had six puppies. Ed and Donna decided to get one of the puppies and name it Bailey. They enjoyed watching Bailey and Danny grow, and it was easy to remember their birthdays!

Danny and Bailey became close friends. They played together and slept together. When Danny went to school, Bailey would always wait at the end of the driveway until he got off the bus. They also celebrated their birthdays together. Danny would invite his friends to the parties, and Bailey would have a few dog visitors as well.

As Bailey got a little older, it became difficult for her to climb the steep stairway to Danny's bedroom. Whenever Danny headed up the stairs, Bailey was right behind, although it took longer than when she was a puppy. Most nights, Bailey would sleep at the foot of Danny's bed, and at times, Bailey would sleep in Ed and Donna's room.

When Bailey reached 13-years-old, she was too old and weak to climb the stairs. Danny would place Bailey's blanket at the foot of the stairs, and there she would sleep until Danny came down in the mornings. Ed and Donna began to worry. They knew Bailey was going to die soon. How would Danny handle it? Ed and Donna feared the day when Bailey would die.

Danny began to realize that Bailey was weak and ill. Not only couldn't she climb the stairs, she could barely walk. Danny had to carry her outside twice a day. One evening in late October, Danny picked her up and placed her on her blanket at the foot of the stairs. He patted her on the head and went upstairs to bed.

At two o'clock in the morning, Danny was awakened. He heard the sounds of small feet coming up the stairs. Who or what could it be? Then he heard the sound on the floor of his room. It was Bailey. She placed her paws on the pillow next to him and licked his face. Then she left his room and went into his parent's room. Bailey went on Donna's side of the bed and kissed her and then she went to the other side of the bed and licked Ed's face. Danny could hear Bailey's little feet hit the steps of the stairway as she headed back down. Danny could not believe what just happened. Was he dreaming? How could this weak and crippled dog climb those stairs?

The next morning, Danny rushed down the stairs as usual to say good morning to Bailey. When he reached her blanket, he found her dead. She had died during the night.

Somehow, Bailey knew she was going to die, and somehow, she gathered enough strength to climb the stairs one more time to kiss her family goodbye. Bailey was determined to climb the stairs and she did it. Determination is a very important skill to master. When you wish to accomplish something, are you determined to reach your goal, or do you let excuses get in the way? Bailey knew she could reach her goal, are you determined to reach yours?

From Monday Morning Messages by Tom Carr (www.youthlight.com)

Teacher, Teacher

By Art Fettig

Teacher, teacher
help me learn
when to press on
when to turn.

Teacher, Teacher
guide my way,
teach me what
I ought to say.

Teacher, Teacher
I'm worthwhile
won't you give me
just one smile?

Teacher, Teacher
you're so grand,
when you help
me understand.

Teacher, Teacher
when you care
you prove love's
a thing we share.

Teacher, Teacher
yes it's true,
Teacher, Teacher
We love you.

Growth

By Art Fettig

I don't ever want to be
what I want to be.

There is always something
out there for me.

I get a kick from living
in the here and now.

Yet, I never want to feel
I've learned the best way how.

There is always one hill higher
with a better view.

Something waiting to be learned
that I never knew.

'til my life is over
never fully fill my cup.

Let me go on growing

Up!
Up!
Up!

Other Books by Tom Carr...

- Keeping Love Alive in the Family

- A Parent's Blueprint

- Monday Morning Messages

- Every Child Has a Gift

- 101 Snake Tales and Bites

- 131 Creative Strategies for Reaching Children With Anger Problems

- Innovative Strategies for Unlocking Difficult Children (co-authored)

REFERENCES

Bettleheim, B. (1987) *The good enough parent*. New York: Random House.

Bowman, R. and Bowman, S. (1998). *The co-piloting mentor program*. Chapin SC: Youthlight, Inc.

Carr, T. (2000). *Every child has a gift*. Chapin SC: Youthlight, Inc.

Carr, T. (2000) *131 creative strategies for reaching children with anger problems*. Chapin, SC: Youthlight Inc.

Carr, T. (1999). *Parents blueprint*. Chapel Hill, NC: Professional Press.

Dodson, T. and Miller, V. (1978). *Aikido in everyday life*. Berkeley, CA: North Atlantic Books.

Garbarino, J. (1999) *Lost boys*. New York: Free Press.

Glasser, W. (1998). *Choice theory*. New York: Harper Collins

Glasser, W. (2000). *Every student can succeed*. Chatsworth, CA: William Glasser, Inc.

Glasser, W. (1965). *Reality therapy*. New York: Harper and Row.

Green, R. (1998). *The explosive child*. New York: Harper Collins.

Halpren, S. (2001). *Four wings and a prayer*. New York: Pantheon Books.

Hecker, L. and Deacon, S. (1998). *The therapist's notebook*. New York: Hawthorn Press.

Jakubowski, P. and Lange, A. (1978). *The assertive option: your rights and responsibilities*. Champaign, IL: Research Press Co.

Jarrett, O. and Maxwell, D. (2000). *What research says about the need for recess. Elementary School Recess* (ed). Clements, R. Boson: American Press.

Jones, F. (1987). *Positive classroom discipline*. New York: McGraw-Hill.

Kohn, A. (1993). *Punished by rewards*. Boston: Houghton Mifflin.

Kohn, A. (1998). *What to look for in a classroom*. San Francisco: Jossey-Bass Publishers.

Kranowitz, C. (1998). *The out-of-sync child*. New York: Berkley Publishing.

Levine, M. (2002). *A mind at a time*. New York: Simon and Schuster.

Lochman, J., Whidby, J. and FitzGerald, D. (2000). *Cognitive-behavioral assessment and treatment with aggressive children*. In Kendall, P (ed.) *Child and adolescent therapy*. New York: Guilford Press.

Lozoff, B. (2000). *It's a meaningful life*. New York: Penguin Putnam.

Payne, R. (2001). *A framework for understanding poverty*. Highlands, TX: Process, Inc.

Prather, H. (1998). *Spiritual notes to myself*. Berkeley, CA: Conari Press.

Queen, J. (1993). *Responsible classroom management*. Charlotte, NC: RCM Associates, Inc.

Steinberg, L. (1996). *Beyond the classroom*. New York: Simon and Schuster.

Sternberg, R. (1996). *Successful intelligence*. New York: Simon and Schuster.